When
Grandma
Wore
Breeches

When Grandma Wore Breeches

Audrey Bagnall

AMBERLEY

May I thank all my family and friends, for their encouragement, their help with photos, and Emily for her animal drawings.

First published 2009

Amberley Publishing Plc
Cirencester Road, Chalford,
Stroud, Gloucestershire, GL6 8PE

www.amberley-books.com

British Library Cataloguing in Publication Data.
A catalogue record for this book is available from the British Library.

ISBN 978 1 84868 235 1

Typesetting and Origination by Amberley Publishing.
Printed in Great Britain.

The Story of a Land Girl

By Audrey Bagnall, née Cross

For my beloved granddaughters,
Emily Louise and Elizabeth Frances

Some names of people and places have been slightly changed
Perhaps some events have been misremembered
These are my own very personal memories of a special time
I was young, it was then that your Grandma wore breeches.

Contents

Foreword

What a joy it was to read Audrey Bagnall's reflections on her years as a member of the Women's Land Army. Her book is written in the form of a diary, chronologically documenting personal anecdotes and memories of individuals, romantic opportunities and a sound knowledge of Dairy Farming during her early life between the ages of seventeen and twenty years old.

Despite covering only three years, Mrs Bagnall's book records the hard, long and laborious work undertaken by the Women's Land Army whose efforts helped to keep our nation fed throughout the challenging years of post-war Britain.

Audrey Bagnall, my own mother and thousands of other women gave so much to so many people during that troubled period and it was a great delight to see these 'unsung heroes' recognised by Her Majesty's government in the same year that this book has been published.

Audrey concludes her book with a wonderful description of what she saw as the attributes of the Land Girls who needed a sense of humour, be able to improvise, ready to tackle anything and know how to enjoy the simplest of pleasures ... her book is a testimony to exactly that!

I congratulate Mrs Bagnall on a skilfully and beautifully constructed account of what was clearly a very important time in her life and in the life of our country and I warmly commend her book to her readers.

Warren J Smith JP
Lord-Lieutenant of Greater Manchester

Chapter One
Spreading of Wings

16 December 1946

The engine hissed in a cloud of steam, the carriage doors slammed, the guard's whistle shrilled – windows were pulled down, hasty 'goodbyes' said, cries of 'write soon' and 'take care' heard. As the great engine started to slide into the darkness beyond the station, I watched from the carriage window as the people on the platform melted out of sight, my Mam among them, her hand still half raised in a wave. The train gathered speed as it headed south towards London. Stowing my kit bag and case on the rack, I settled in my seat; I could hardly believe that it was only a few short weeks since I had gone into Manchester on my half day and on seeing the posters in the W.L.A office, I had ventured inside.

At sixteen I was looking for a change, I wanted to travel, spread my wings; the Women's Services were the obvious choice, some of the uniforms were very smart. However, being of an independent nature, I did not relish the thought of regimentation, marching and drilling. Generally the age of recruitment was eighteen, but for the Womens' Land Army it was, with parents' consent, seventeen; my birthday was only a few weeks away!

The colourful posters, sunny harvest fields, and smiling Land Girls with their arms full of golden sheaves of corn rather appealed to me. I got an application form. On offer was 'Field Work', 'General Farmwork', 'Forestry' and 'Dairying'. I made the latter my preference. The starting wage was 18/9 (92 pence) per week, plus board and lodgings.

The bombshell landed when I asked my Mam and Dad to give their consent to me joining. They thought the work would be much too heavy for me; being an only child they thought I would be mixing with, shall I say, rough elements. Why should I want to leave the local high class shop where I had gone to work on leaving school at fourteen? My wage at the shop had been 15 shillings per week (75 pence), with half a crown (12½ pence) rise each birthday. My seventeenth birthday brought my wage to the princely sum of 22/6 a week, which, I must add, was pretty poor even in those days.

A poster from the time encouraging women to join the Land Army.

*A poster from the time encouraging women to join the
Land Army.*

Eventually, I wore Dad down and he reluctantly consented. I attended a medical with our own family doctor, accompanied by my Mam who expressed her thoughts about my suitability for the Land Army, and indeed the Land Army's suitability for me. To which the doctor looked at me (I am sure he winked) and said 'don't worry mother, it will do her the world of good.' So that was my medical, and to think how Mam had fussed over me having a bath and putting on my best underwear for the occasion.

On another half day I attended an interview, and when asked why I wanted to do dairy work I replied that I would like to work with animals. It was stressed that it could be a seven days a week job, together with early morning starts. It was very demanding work.

'What the heck,' I thought, and with a flourish I signed on the dotted line for two years service.

It was quite exciting waiting for my uniform to arrive. When I tried it on, a different person looked back at me from the bedroom mirror, wearing a cream shirt, green pullover and a green tie. The fawn corduroy breeches were hard to put on, with laces below the knee, three buttons either side of the waist and a leather belt. The uniform also consisted of fawn three-quarter length woollen socks and brown lace up shoes. I was also the proud owner of an overcoat, hat, dungarees and wellington boots. I clomped downstairs to show Mam and Dad, they said that they looked nice warm things, Dad gave me his advice 'to put my name on all my belongings, and not to be too trusting.' Whether he meant with my possessions or where young men were concerned, I do not know. Perhaps he meant both!

Now I was officially W.L.A. 178403, and I awaited my posting, Then the brown envelope landed on the mat. The contents gave details of an eight-week course in hand milking and dairy work commencing on 16 December at Limpsfield near Oxted, Surrey. The envelope also contained a railway warrant with instructions of an early morning, four-and-a-half hour train journey from London Road (now called Piccadilly), Manchester to Euston, London. The journey was to continue by train to Oxted via Victoria, followed by a bus to Limpsfield, and finally a quarter-hour walk to 'Limpsfield Lodge', arriving in the early afternoon.

When it came to handing in my notice and telling the boss that I had joined the Land Army, he insisted he did not want to lose me before Christmas and I was offered a move up the promotion ladder, while my wage would go up to 35/- a week. However, by now I had the bit between my teeth and said that, as I had signed up for 2 years, I could hardly go back on my word. I was promised my job back if I wanted to return. My friends on the staff presented me with their good wishes and an "Antler" weekend case as a leaving gift. I began to wonder if I had done the right thing as I was going to miss everyone, but it was too late now for doubts to creep in, and I was on my way.

As it became light thick whirling flakes of snow started to fall, and as the train began to slow down, I looked out of the carriage window and could see huddled groups of Italian Prisoners of War clearing the lines and frozen points; they had fires burning in braziers. As the train slid past them, I felt as alien in my surroundings as they probably did, being so far from their homeland. At Rugby more passengers joined the train and I spotted a girl in W.L.A uniform. Her name was Mary and we joined forces when we found that we were both going to the same destination. Unfortunately the train was a few hours late getting into Euston, so we thought it would be better to get a taxi to Victoria, as we had no understanding of London buses or the Underground. When I saw the hustle and bustle crossing London, I felt that the extravagance of the shared taxi fare was a good investment. We had a long cold wait for a train to Oxted and when we got there it was dark and still snowing. We found a bus that dropped us off at Limpsfield, but worried that the remaining directions of a 'quarter of an hour's' walk to Limpsfield Lodge were a little daunting. On enquiring the way to go, the locals looked at us, our pile of luggage and the fast falling snow, and told us we had better try to get a taxi to come out from Oxted, if we wanted to get to 'Titsey' that night.

After yet another long wait for the taxi to arrive, we lurched and bumped up a narrow lane until the beam of the car's headlights lit up a gateway, and a house loomed up through the whirling snow. We could see long low lines of buildings and flickering lamps, and could hear cattle lowing and girls' voices. We were wet, cold and hungry and so glad to get into the house. The wardens met us; they were two sisters, both kindly ladies, and one thing that struck me immediately was when we were told 'there was no electricity'. It was a world of open fires and tilly lamps, while a glowing kitchen range produced the good smell of food. By candlelight we were shown upstairs to where our beds were, and after dumping our things, came down for tea to meet the other girls who were coming in from work. There seemed to be so many of them, with red cheeks, red noses and even redder hands – big jolly girls, shy girls, some very friendly, others quiet. In all, there were about a dozen girls in the space of the living room hearth rug – it was all rather overwhelming. Some girls came from Yorkshire, some from Liverpool, several from Manchester, a small dark girl was from Wales, and a few came from Surrey. We were, it seemed, a very mixed bunch! The evening meal was served in the living room, because it was too cold in the dining room. It was a happy mealtime, lit by the firelight and the tilly lamp.

Winter 1946–47 at Limpsfield Lodge

Everyone laughed at the supposed 'quarter of an hour's walk' to the lodge, and it was speculated that whoever had written those directions had never tried it at the end of a long journey with luggage to carry. Mary and I asked about the name of the place and were told it was 'Titsey Hill', but the W.L.A had renamed it 'Limpsfield Lodge' to save our blushes. After tea the girls followed their own pursuits; I went up the back stairs, which were nearest to the bedroom I was sharing. There were four or five interconnecting bedrooms and another staircase at the front. The floors were plain wooden boards, the beds were wooden with the head and foot folded under for stacking, the mattress was a bit thin, and the bedclothes rather sparse. I had a small wardrobe and a drawer in a dressing table, sharing the room with three other girls.

Mary, my travelling companion was in another room, which I was a bit sorry about. There was no heating upstairs and the window pane was a lacey picture of frosty ferns. I melted a peep hole with the candle and I could see that the outside world was blanketed in thick snow. Little did we know then that the winter of 1946–47 was to go on record as one of the longest, harshest and coldest winters of the last century.

On unpacking my case, I found my Mam had put in a hot water bottle for me. I took out my new writing case and by candlelight wrote my first letter home. Downstairs I could hear the girls laughing and singing. I went down to join them and had my leg pulled when I was told that my first milking lesson was to be on Victor, who I found out was the bull!

On going to bed a girl called Sylvia, who came from the Hulme area of Manchester, was in a bed near me. I could not help but wonder if she was very shy, as she got into bed wearing all her underwear and socks. She then proceeded to wriggle out of her things under the bedclothes, and put them under her pillow. I, meanwhile, undressed and neatly folded my things by the side of the bed. We blew out the candles said 'Good night, God bless', before I turned over and there was a tremendous crash! My bed end had collapsed. In the dark and a fit of giggles I repaired the damage and added my overcoat to the bedding. So, I had arrived at Limpsfield. I cuddled Mam's hot water bottle and fell asleep, wondering what on earth I was doing here, when I could have been at home in my own little room.

It was the middle of the night, someone was shaking me and telling me to get up. It was Dolly, she was the senior Land Girl and saw to it that everyone was awake. She dashed through the bedrooms, lighting candles, and waking us up. My watch showed 5.40 am, the other girls were stirring and Sylvia did a complete reversal of the previous night's routine. She emerged from under the bed clothes needing only her overalls and boots. As I shivered into my cold clothes, I realised modesty wasn't the reason that Sylvia dressed and undressed in bed, instead it was so she had a warm start to her day!

She told me to just have a wee and not to bother with a wash until breakfast time, because you got your face chapped. Sylvia knew a thing or two!

Everyone went outside to the sheds and the air was as keen as a knife, taking your breath away. We had to dig the snow away from the shed doors before we could get them to open. The sheds adjoined large partly covered yards and the cows were let in from the yards to take their place for milking. The great steaming beasts came lumbering in; each one knew her own stall and woe betide any cow that ventured into her neighbour's place when the rightful occupant arrived.

My first very important lesson I had in dairying was to 'keep out of the way' as the cattle came past, their eyes rolling and horns tossing. When they were in their places, we had to squeeze between the cows and fasten their neck chains. It was then I realised how warm cows are! Buckets, stools and scales were brought from the dairy and set up, alongside some cloths and warmish water. My next lesson was to wash the cow's udder, while keeping a look out if she started to lift her tail and get to one side sharpish if you did not want splattering. To cheers from the girls, mugs of hot steaming tea arrived. I don't think I have ever tasted tea as good before, or since. The milking continued in a flurry; cows were washed, girls sat milking, and milk was weighed and recorded and then taken to the dairy. Here it went over the cooler and was measured into 10 or 12 gallon churns to be collected by the milk lorry. The non-milkers went outside into the yards to put hay into the racks for the cows when they came out again after milking. I did not know the difference between hay and straw, but soon found out that straw is the dried corn stalks used for bedding. Hay, on the other hand, was dried grass for the animals to eat and it also came in useful to line your boots and wellingtons as it generates warmth. Victor the bull and the young stock needed food and water, but the icy conditions made hard work of everything. It was 8 am by the time we went into breakfast; I felt that I had done a day's work already and it was barely coming light.

Chapter Two
Limpsfield Lodge

Breakfast was a time to get a proper wash and make your bed. That mine of useful information, Sylvia, told me never to leave anything on the bedroom floor, as the Swiss cleaning lady threw anything and everything into a sack in the boot room. It was no use to inquire where your things might have gone, as she refused to speak English.

When we went outside again, Mrs Mac, the herdswoman, set us to work, and set some of the girls to cleaning the dairy. I was with the girls doing the sheds. The dung had to be shovelled up out of the gutters and barrowed outside. It was somewhat hazardous pushing a barrowful to the tip, and one girl slipped in those icy conditions and she and the load ended in a smelly heap. The sheds were swept and swilled clean. The job the girls detested, especially in that awful cold weather, was troughing, which entailed scrubbing out each stone trough with cold water, with even colder hands. My hands became so numb and cold that even though I had knocked skin off my knuckles, I didn't feel it till my hands got warm again. When the sheds were done, to Dolly's satisfaction, we had to carry tubs of silage and tip them into the clean troughs ready for the cows when they came in for the afternoon milking. As we were given a tub we were told the name of the cow it was for, as the amount varied as to how she was milking. We got familiar with the cows names – they all began with 'L,' for Limpsfield – we had Lupin, Larry, Lydia, and so on, not forgetting Lu-Lu, she was notorious for kicking and most girls landed in the gutter when they went to wash her. I think she had been roughly treated at sometime and it took a brave soul to milk her.

A tractor was working out on the lane, and by dinner time the milk lorry, with chains on its wheels, had managed to crawl up the lane, welcomed with cheers from us. It was good to see something from the outside world.

After dinner, several of us went up the hill behind the farm, crunching through the untouched snow, dragging a wooden sledge. From the hill you could see the surrounding woods and the countryside, and far below us the house, farm buildings and everything else wore a deep mantle of crisp snow. Overhead the cloudless sky was a deep blue and everywhere sparkled in the sun. We flattened down a 'toboggan run' and as the first two girls launched off down the hill, we cheered them on their way. We threw snowballs and made a snowman. Rich holiday makers in the Alps could not have enjoyed themselves more than we did. We went back to work, laughing and tingling.

During the afternoon milking, I had my first attempt at milking, perched on a little three-legged stool, with a bucket between my ankles. I tried a few tentative squirts, as I had been shown. The patient cow looked round at me, munched her silage and gave such a very long sigh, as if to resign herself to yet another learner. Her next door neighbour decided to lean on me. So there I sat, sandwiched between two great cows, my shoulder being flapped with two tails. I got quite a few squirts out of the teats, enough to cover the bottom of the bucket. That was enough for one day and I relinquished my perch to a more experienced milker to complete the job. When the afternoon milking was complete, the feeding and watering done, the dairy attended to and the cows were out in the yards again, at last we had finished. It was wonderful to get indoors out of the cold and dark.

We left our wellingtons in the boot room and we padded around in slippers or woolly socks. A warm meal inside, and sat in a warm room; I could hardly keep my eyes open. Someone wound up the gramophone (which had been donated by the readers of the *Daily Mail*) and I heard for the first, and certainly not the last time, the only record we had to play on it! One side was 'Marie's Wedding', a jolly Scottish song and the other side of the record played 'Ta rang Bolang', a sad Maori farewell.

After these had been played a couple of times each, someone tried the wireless set. The battery was nearly flat and it would require a journey into Oxted to get it recharged, so we did not bother with it. We spent our evenings reading, writing letters, washing, ironing, or sitting round the fire talking about our homes, our families, our boyfriends, and singing. We sang everything: Christmas carols; popular songs of the day and wartime favourites that we all knew. There were even some songs I had never heard before, or since. We used to choose a song each and debate the order we would sing them in – it all had to be fair! As I ended my first day in the Land Army, I rolled into bed in my underwear and took a leaf out of Sylvia's book. I dread to think what my Mam would have thought of me; was it only yesterday that I had arrived? I already felt as if I had done a week's work and lived in another world. As we said 'Goodnight' and blew out the candles, we knew the snow was softly falling again. All too soon Dolly would be round to wake us up and we would have to dig our way into the sheds again in the morning. I slept like a log.

Life settled into a routine and I felt better when letters started to arrive from home. I was always happy to see the little red mail van wending its way up the lane. There is something so very special about a letter; opening it and knowing that it had been written with a loving hand, you read it then kept it in your pocket to treasure, to read and re-read again. I must admit that I used to put my letters under my pillow at night, as it made me feel home was not quite so far away.

One day Mary told me that she was not staying in the Land Army and that she was packing up and going home for Christmas. She said she would not live in these rough conditions. Asking if I was staying, I could not give leaving a moment's thought having made such an effort to join. I just could not go home defeated after a week. I would never have lived it down back at work or home; and anyway, I did not have the train fare.

Keeping clean was something of a problem, as being an only child and a bit shy, it took some getting used to sharing the bathroom. There was not an abundance of hot water and if several of us were going out we even had to share the one bath. It was a downstairs bathroom and the window was not as frosted as it might have been, so we used to drape a sheet over the window in case the local lads were around! Despite this they always teased us that they knew who had been in the bathroom. I recalled Florence Nightingale's theory, that given privacy and a couple of pints of water, a woman will keep herself clean. I used to get a kettle of hot water and have a strip wash, starting at the top and working down. It is surprising how far that drop of water went – I even washed my socks in what was left!

Washing our clothes was such a problem; the water was hard and soap was rationed. We sent our overalls and shirts to the laundry, but we had to handwash our personal things. It was impossible to get things dry outside, even if during the day it might be fine and sunny, because everything froze solid. We then hung clothes in the boot room until they had some of the wet out of them, then they were brought into the kitchen last thing at night to dry off.

Period times were a great problem, the cold weather gave me tummy ache and at those times I longed for a warm drink, a couple of tablets, and a lie down with a hot water bottle. Sanitary towels (or S.T.s as we referred to them) were not as they are now as they were very scarce and expensive, costing about 1/8*d* to 2 shillings a packet, with one packet being insufficient for the month. A lot of ladies used to have washable towels which were pinned on, or we made some for ourselves with loops and an elastic belt. Used S.T.s had to be burnt, hidden at the back of fire in the kitchen range. A few girls used tampons but they were not popular and it was considered not quite 'lady-like' to use those. Mind you, the harrowing tales that Sylvia related to the times her sister lost the string were enough to put any one off.

Ironing was another trial; as we had no electricity we used flat irons, and you needed two on the go – one in use and one heating up on the front of the fire.

Although the Land Army uniform was standard, girls soon put their own touches to what they wore. If you cut out the sleeves from discarded old pullovers and applied the minimum of stitching, you had an extra pair of socks to go in your wellingtons. If the remaining body part was any good, you could wear it back-to-front, under your working pullover. That was a lot warmer and saved wearing a shirt. Then there was 'the hat', that gave scope for individuality. I remember a very happy evening in the kitchen at Limpsfield steaming our hats; we got more shapes out of those basic brown felt hats than one would think possible. My hat ended up in the 'cowboy' style complete with a leather bootlace and toggle to fasten it under the chin. I was pleased with the end result and always wore my hat at a jaunty angle when I was going out.

The only photo of the author wearing breeches.
Note the two pullovers; one on back to front
for warmth and to save washing

Boyfriends and sex was a subject we talked about, or 'going all the way'. It seemed that above the waist was fairly safe, but below the waist was fraught with danger. I understood that, if a couple were to be adventurous, a 'rubber' sheath was a must. These were obtained by the boyfriend from the chemist's or the barber's shop; they cost two shillings and six pence (half a crown) for three. This was quite expensive; I heard of them being washed and re-rolled to economise. Sylvia gave dire warnings not to get 'carried away' and allow the boyfriend to go too far and disregard his reassurances that 'he would get off at Crewe', so before you knew it you would have 'gone all the way to Manchester!' If he were to contact 'the little man in the boat' you were sunk!

Apparently Sylvia's sister had some very anxious times when her period was late after her boyfriend had been home on leave. It was a relief all round when it was a 'false alarm.' That poor girl; everything seemed to happen to her, so I took a warning from her experiences.

I just cinched my leather belt around my twenty-two inch waist and laced my breeches firmly below the knees. I felt all was safely gathered in; a maid I was and a maid I was going to stay, for the foreseeable future.

Christmas was soon upon us. We enjoyed ourselves, although the work had to go on. Several of us went to the Christmas Eve service, singing carols all the way. Over Christmas we paid a few visits to The Bull and had snowball fights with the local lads. When they were out numbered and getting the worst of it, Pax was called and they gave us a lift back up the lane on their motor bikes. We once managed to get five on a Harley Davidson. One young man, Brian, was sweet on me and presented me with a head scarf as I was to be his pillion. It was exciting to roar off down the lanes, holding close and swaying the bends together. Miss Dan and Mrs Mac turned a blind eye over the Christmas holidays when some of the lads came up to help us feed the stock and do some of the chores so that we could finish earlier. Then we all went up the hill sledging, again, I do not know what my Mam would have thought if she had seen me. Going downhill on the sledge with Brian, we got up such a speed that we overshot and would have gone through the barbed wire fence at the bottom if we hadn't rolled off and landed in a laughing heap. It was all innocent fun.

New Year came and brought no respite from the biting cold of that terrible winter. Letters from home told of the shortage of fuel; coal was rationed and people queued at the Gas Works to buy coke. One morning, when bringing in the cows, we found a beautiful snowy owl, but it was dead and frozen. I pondered on what icy wastes it must have crossed, driven down from its homeland by the bitter winds. I was sad that such a beautiful creature had perished. It was a cruel time for man and beast.

In that great white world there was unforgettable beauty. I remember a row of tall poplars; during the day the snow had melted on them, only to suddenly freeze as the day was ending. Every trunk, branch and twig of the trees were coated in a crystal shell of ice, and as the great red winter sun set behind them they glowed as if they were on fire. If only I had colour films and a camera then ... what scenes I could have captured.

Some of the senior girls were soon getting posted out to farms. I was sorry to lose Sylvia. She tossed me an extra blanket off her bed before she went; I was going to miss her, the laughs, and the good common sense she had. I had the feeling that Sylvia was one of the 'rougher elements' my Mam had wished me to avoid. A few new girls arrived and we always had a laugh at the 'quarter of an hour's walk' – it became a standing joke. I found myself as one of the old hands, and after several weeks on basic Land Army pay, I came on a better wage of about 30s a week. This was paid by the Surrey War Agricultural Executive Committee, or S.W.A.E.C. I think Mam and Dad were quite impressed when I wrote home, as it was a substantial pay rise.

We had lectures on dairy work from Miss Dan. By this time I had got the knack of hand milking. At first the muscles in my forearms ached, then they got rock hard. It became a badge of pride as to how firm your muscles were! To be able to milk a cow on a cold winter morning is a nice warm experience. I used to talk to her and lean my head against her flank so she would relax and 'let down' her milk. It would start to flow and you got a steady rhythm going. The milk makes a different sound when it first hits the bottom of the bucket to when you have a gallon or more; then it becomes a rich 'whooshing' sound. If you have milked well there is a good froth on the top.

As I got more experienced I got a bit mischievous. The farm cats would sit on the other side of the gutter across from the cows and with a well aimed backward squirt of the cows teat, you could reach the cats. Some were good at catching the milk in their mouths, while some even stood up on their hind legs, open mouthed. If they missed they sat there washing their bibs until next time.

When I had a weekend off one time, I was unable to return home as the round trip took so long – I had to be back in time for next week's work. Another girl, Jane, was also off that weekend. She lived in Plaistow in London and she kindly invited me to go home with her. Jane's family lived in a sort of basement flat, and they made me very welcome.

On the Saturday evening we all went to their local pub. We were a jolly crowd and we had a sing-song while the pianist pounded out the popular tunes. Two naval officers joined our company, and when one was found to come from 'up North' they hutched up and sat him next to me! We chatted and he came from Bolton; William was his name. By the end of the evening he walked me to Jane's door and we lingered outside. It was a clear frosty night and he pointed out the names of brilliant stars and constellations. It was bitterly cold; I felt myself tremble, but it was not with cold. Our breaths mingled in the frosty air and I knew that I had found someone very special. Before we parted he insisted on having my address. I don't know what my Mam would have thought if she had known that I had just received a proposal of marriage and was being tenderly kissed goodnight by a man I had just met! William and his pal wended their way to the Y.M.C.A. to get a bed for the night, as they were going back to the submarine base at Gosport the next day. I had to share Jane's bed and we whispered and giggled together. Jane was older than me, being about twenty and more worldly wise, and told me 'he won't write, they never do!'

A farm cat

The next morning it was marvellous to be woken up by Jane's mother with a cup of tea at 9 am. Jane showed me around London, and we jumped on and off buses and went up and down the Underground. We went to Speakers' Corner, listening to people putting the world right from their soap boxes. It was all great fun.

When went back to Limpsfield again on Sunday night, Jane and the girls pulled my leg mercilessly about my 'romance'. Much to everyone's amazement, but somehow not mine, I received a letter on Tuesday morning written in a bold hand bearing a Gosport postmark. It was a lovely letter and many more followed.

Life in the Land Army could be hazardous and I got somewhat 'battle scarred'. On one occasion, several of us were sent up the fields with the tractor and a trailer full of dung to be spread. One girl was too close to me and caught my face with her fork. I was lucky not to have lost my eye. Miss Dan took me to the Cottage Hospital, where I was cleaned up.

It left me with a scar on my cheek and while it was healing I was kept away from the milking, doing dairy and other jobs. This lead to me going to feed some young stock on my own. They were very hungry and jostled me, so much so that one heifer caught her horn at the bottom of my back. It broke the skin and two years later I needed an operation to put it right. Two or three of us should have done the job, keeping the animals back until the food was in the trough.

Ellen and I both had our afternoon off, so we caught the bus to Croydon. She had been chaining up a cow and it had tossed its head at the wrong time and Ellen ended up with a black eye and a bump on her nose. I had the scar on my face too, so when we blithely went shopping in Croydon everyone kept looking at us. We collapsed in a fit of giggles on the return bus when we asked for two tickets to Titsey Corner.

Several new girls arrived and among them was Lorna Jackson who I became good friends with. She was a real tomboy, a good worker and smashing company. She had been born in Australia, but her parents had come back home to England and the family lived in Liverpool. It was not long before we were moving her bed and belongings into the bedroom I was in.

The time came for me to take the milking exam, where I had to hand milk two cows. I choose Larry and Lydia, two that I liked, as they were good natured and I hoped that they liked me – the last thing I wanted was a foot in the bucket. While the examiner watched me I felt quite posh in an unaccustomed white coat and, ignoring the farm cats waiting hopefully, I recorded and weighed the milk. The examiner had a look at the cows to see if they were stripped out properly, and as he was satisfied with the job, I had passed and was now ready for posting to pastures new.

One day Miss Dan had a word with me as there was a posting that had come in that she thought might suit me very well. I was to go for an interview with Mr Hunt, the farm bailiff at Merrist Wood, the Surrey Farm Institute at Worplesdon, near Guildford.

Lorna Jackson

Chapter Three
Merrist Wood

I got off the bus at the New Inn, Worplesdon and following directions I crossed the road heading for a lane. My heels rang out on the road and I felt a spring to my step; it was so much warmer, the snow was melting, the trickle of running water was in the ditches, birds chirped and flitted in the hedge rows. At last winter was slowly easing its icy grip on the land. It was the end of March and my thoughts turned to my interview with the farm bailiff; I hoped he would not be a tartar to work for.

I came to a pair of big iron gates which stood wide open and to one side were a number of lovely black and white farm cottages. There was also a stable court yard and buildings – 'This looks like it,' I thought – but on asking for Mr Hunt I was told he would be up 'the House'. Continuing along the lane, past a clump of tall fir trees, I turned a bend and I got my first sight of Merrist Wood Hall. It was a fine house, perhaps built a hundred years before, in a black and white mock Tudor style. From an open window came the chatter of many voices and the clatter of cutlery from what sounded like a dining room. I was apprehensive at approaching the huge stone porch, wondering if I should have gone to find the back entrance. Suddenly the door opened and a gentleman greeted me: 'Hello! You must be my new Land Girl.' This was Mr Hunt.

Going into his office, he told me that they had a herd of Dairy Shorthorns, about 60 in milk, and an Alpha Laval milking bale. I told him I had only done hand milking and had no experience at all of machine milking. He brushed this aside as a matter of no importance at all, assuring me that I would soon pick it up. Miss Dan had recommended me and that was good enough far him. He told me that if I came over on Sunday afternoon, then I could start work Monday morning. Evidently, here was a man who gave his orders and expected the job done.

I agreed, and indeed hoped that I would 'soon pick it up'.

When it came to leaving Limpsfield, I did not realise how much I had come to feel an affection for the place. The girls that had come and gone, all the laughs, some tears, the comradeship, the songs, the farm cats and the herd, my special cows – even Lu-Lu wasn't that bad. I would miss the wardens and local people that had been friendly to me, including Brian's mother who was the landlady of The Bull, who had tactfully never asked our ages. I gave my new address to friends and we parted promising to write and keep in touch.

Sunday found me making my way up the lane to Merrist Wood again, this time with my kitbag on my shoulder and carrying my case. I found that I was staying in 'the House'. On being shown to my room I could not believe my eyes; it was so warm and spacious with two windows, both with lovely views over gardens and the fields beyond. What a treat lay in store, after the Spartan conditions at Limpsfield. There was electricity, central heating and a girls' bathroom along the landing, with two baths and washbasins with lashings of hot water!

Merrist Wood Hall in spring 1947

I was sharing the room with Pat, the other Land Girl. She was friendly and made me feel welcome. I felt shy going down to the dining room for the evening meal, but only a few people were there as it was a Sunday. The room had previously been the Billiards room; it still retained a few shaded lamps, but now there were about a dozen tables each seating six or eight. Everyone kept to their regular table and Pat and I sat together.

That evening, lots of people seemed to arrive to the sound of doors banging, laughing, music and the clatter of many feet. In my room I wrote a letter home; it seemed strange giving my new address 'Merrist Wood Hall', and I wondered what Mam and Dad would think.

I unpacked my things and, with some trepidation, laid out my working clothes for morning. I had joined the Land Army looking for change and I had certainly found it. Tomorrow I had the prospect of meeting seventy or more people, sixty cows and that Alpha Laval milking bale.

Pat woke me up about 5.30 am and she gathered up three square boxes which she told me were the 'pulsators' to the bale. If they were left in the sheds they froze, so she looked after them. We went downstairs, made a cup of tea in the kitchen, had a slice of bread and then went out to the boot room. Pat was going down to the sheds on her bike, and she pointed across the fields for me to make my way over a stile, keeping to the path, and told me to look for the lights. I felt so alone, it was still dark and so very cold. What a relief it was when I saw the shadowy outline of buildings and lights coming on ahead of me. Then I could hear the cows and that was at least one familiar, friendly sound.

We started milking at 6 am. Leo was the herdsman; he and Pat did the milking while I was back again at the business end washing cows' udders and taking samples in the strip cup to make sure the cows were clear of mastitis before they went on the machines.

As it started to come light the rest of the farm staff started work. It appeared that the milking sheds were a popular meeting place, as workers left their milk cans in the dairy. Mr Hunt popped in to see how we were doing, along with the Pig Man and his dog, and three tractor drivers who arrived and put their motor bikes in an empty loose box. The five students that had overslept and were on the milking group that day eventually arrived, too. There was the boiler to stoke, which looked like a monster with a mind of its own. By 8 am the milk lorry arrived to be loaded and on its way. The clatter of the tail board dropping and men's voices, '*guten morgen*' heralded the arrival of the German Prisoners-of-War in their lorry.

After breakfast, Pat and I went down to the sheds to do the dairy, which consisted of scrubbing everything and putting it into the steriliser. We blasted everything with steam and held the temperature at 212 degrees Fahrenheit for at least 10 minutes. The bale itself was pumped through with cold water and cleaning solution, before being rinsed and then steamed to sterilise it. It was not as daunting as I feared, in fact it was a doddle.

Pat told me that the milking bale was quite new and there had been a lot of teething problems with it over the winter. Pat was good to work with as she explained things to me. She was about 25, and appeared a little studious behind her glasses and looked as if she would rather read the *Farmers' Weekly* than *Women's Own*.

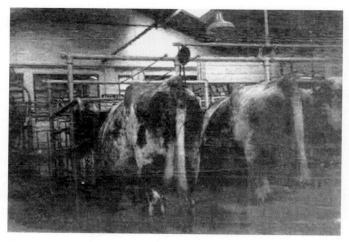

The cows inside the Alpha Laval milking bale, Merrist Wood 1947

The afternoon found me on the milking side of the bale; we let the students do the moving and washing of the cows as they had been late in that morning. I found myself in charge of one milking machine. The cows came through and had their rations of cattle cake dispensed to them from a hopper. The milk was pumped into big glass jars hung on a weighing device, ten pounds to a gallon, and when the cow was finished, Pat showed me how to strip out the last drop of milk. Then with a turn of a handle that milk went through the pipes and into the dairy over the cooler. I needed to get know the cows and their names to record their production. The afternoon milking was done with a 'donkey engine' providing power. We did have an electric motor, but it was unreliable due to power cuts. If that happened the vacuum was lost and clusters would fall off, upsetting the cows. We fed the calves and the bull and left hay and silage for the cows, then finished.

There was a chorus of 'Goodnight' and *'gute Nacht'* as every one wended, trundled or roared their way homeward.

Evening meal was at 6 pm and I had time to have a lovely warm bath and get changed; I must say I wallowed. Of the students there were only six girls, so the bathroom was never overcrowded. After the meal there was a 'quiet hour' for the students to study and write up their day's notes, so no radios or gramophones were allowed. Pat and I fell in with this and we read or wrote our letters at the same time. I got Pat to make a list of all the cows' names for me to memorise. The herd were all named after flowers. As I rolled into bed, at the end of my first day, I felt it had gone well and wondered whether perhaps Dad could send my bike down for me!

Again life began to take on a pattern. I got to know the students, as a different group came down to the sheds each day, along with the farm staff and the P.O.W.s when they collected their milk cans from the dairy and the staff in the House, as we ate and lived together. There was, however, one thing that had slipped to the back of my mind. Pat announced that we would 'Strip the bale down this morning'. 'Good heavens!', I thought. 'We're not going to take that lot apart surely?' Being brought up on the notion that, if a thing was working, it should be left well enough alone, I really hoped she knew what she was doing as she set about the pipe work with a big spanner. The table in the dairy was covered in various lengths of chrome tubing, gaskets, washers, rubber seals, screws and nuts. The fittings on the three large glass jars all came apart by using a special tool. I wondered if we would get it all reassembled for the afternoon milking or would we back to hand milking? The clusters of cups all came apart and had rubber liners which we had to check and renew if needed. It was like a giant Meccano set! I had visions of there being no dinner for us that day as we set about reassembling it all. The test came when it was all rinsed through and we started up the engine. It worked! The pulsators throbbed like beating hearts, there were no leaks on the joints and the vacuum held. We were in good time for dinner.

Dad sent my bike by railway for me, it was wonderful. I took off the packing and I went for a spin up and down the lane – freedom. I could ride down to the sheds with Pat or to the village, even Guildford was within reach. I was Queen of the road now!

Lorna and I exchanged letters regularly; she told of the plane crash on the hill which had known such laughter that winter, that she was due to take her milking exam and was soon to be posted. Most of the girls I had known had got scattered over the county. Limpsfield was now full of new girls.

Chapter Four

Springtime

Life was so much easier for everyone as the winter was giving way to spring, and what a spring! It was as though nature, so long held back, was revelling in the warmth of the sun and the lengthening days. Merrist had its own woodlands; it looked as though great drifts of snow were still lingering under the trees, but they were swathes of snowdrops followed by nodding daffodils and, later, the haze of bluebells. I loved to have a walk in the woods that were so rich with wildlife. If you were quiet the rabbits came out, there was a badger set, grey squirrels and birds; so many different ones I had never seen or heard before.

The fields also were transformed and the tractors and horses were out working all the daylight hours disking, drilling and harrowing. A green haze would cover a field and soon the little shoots would be ankle high, as the crops appeared. Nature was indeed bountiful.

Working at Merrist, I had become an employee of Surrey County Council. Our hours averaged 58-60 hours a week (harvest time was 70 hours) and we had to work Saturdays and Sundays, but we took a full week day off. I'd never had spare money before, but now I was able to put a few pounds away in a Post Office book. After my board and lodging of 25*d.* was paid I had around 50*d.* (£2.50) to keep or spend! The Herdsman chose to have Tuesdays off, as that was Guildford market day while Pat went home on Wednesday; I did not mind and either Thursday or Friday suited me. I loved my day off; I always had a shampoo and bath the night before and a lie in until 8 am for breakfast, then I was off to sample the delights of Guildford or meet up with friends from Limpsfield, criss-crossing the county on the Greenline buses or on Southern Railway. These trains had 'Ladies Only' compartments, but I did not use those as I was more than happy to enjoy the company of my fellow travellers. I once boarded the train for East Grinstead and found myself with a number of young men, in R.A.F. uniforms who introduced themselves as 'McIndoe's Guinea Pigs.'

So many young men suffered terrible injuries when planes crashed in flames, and these men were having their shattered faces and hands rebuilt with pioneering plastic surgery. What men they were; one could not help but feel a deep sense of compassion for them, but they just wanted a young girl to look at them, smile, and join in their banter.

One morning, on Pat's day off, I was rattling away in the dairy singing to myself. Leo came in for a bucket of warm water, and asked me to leave the dairy and come to help him. We went round to the pens, and going inside I saw a cow, in some distress, staggering and panting. Leo was a good stockman and he had a lifetime's understanding of animals. When the cow turned I could see a calf's leg coming out under her tail. Leo had to lather his hand and arm and investigate. I gathered that the head was not lying as it should and he was trying to sort out several legs. I just did as I was told, and found myself holding on to a pair of brand new hooves. 'Don't let them go back, when she heaves again just ease downward with her', he said. A wet warm nose appeared, then a little tongue was licking my hand. 'Right now, here we come'; a wet steaming bundle landed at my feet. 'Wipe its nose and mouth, move it over there'. 'Here we are old girl'. With a mighty heave and a bellow from the cow, out came the twin. It was the first calving I had seen; what a delight it was to see the cow nuzzling her calves. We helped her to dry them, rubbing them with handfuls of hay. Soon they tottered to their feet and Leo put them to the mother's udder. The calves were beautiful, each one was dark red with a matching white blaze on the forehead. Mr Hunt came into the pens, asking what we had got. Leo told him it was a couple of nice heifers. Later, I was told that if the twins had been a bull and heifer they would both have gone to market, as the belief was that the female, called a Freemartin, would be a 'poor doer' when it came to breeding.

Leo brought out the Herd Book and inscribed the date and details of Magnolia the 3rd and 4th. They took their mother's herd name. Their sire was our own bull, Sweet William, or his pedigree name of Wendiss Warrior.

As I completed my dairy, I felt that life was so worthwhile when surrounded by the warm spring air and the abundance of new life.

No Test Match wicket could have had a more thorough inspection than that field. Was the fence sound? Was the water laid on? Had the ground dried out enough? As for the grass, the great debate ranged over the differing qualities of meadow mixtures, bents, ryes, fescues and red and white clover. Wise heads nodded and pipes were puffed in agreement. 'Yes, today we will let the cows out!' The yard doors were cleared and thrown open; the cows knew something different was afoot and started a commotion of mooing and bellowing.

The herd had been indoors all those long, cold winter months and they sniffed the warmer air and the smell of fresh, lush grass. Goodness me, some were so eager, others a bit tentative, as we guided them to the field. Then the uproar really began. William could see his 'girls' and he joined in the din while the younger cows put their tails in the air and galloped round and round the field. The mood was infectious and even the more sedate matrons joined in, huge bags swinging. We all leaned on the gate enjoying the fun until the herd settled to graze. Then we returned to our tasks, smiling and feeling that winter was conquered and we had the wonderful promise of summer days ahead.

The cows coming in for milking

The author with young stock Nortons, Merrist 1947

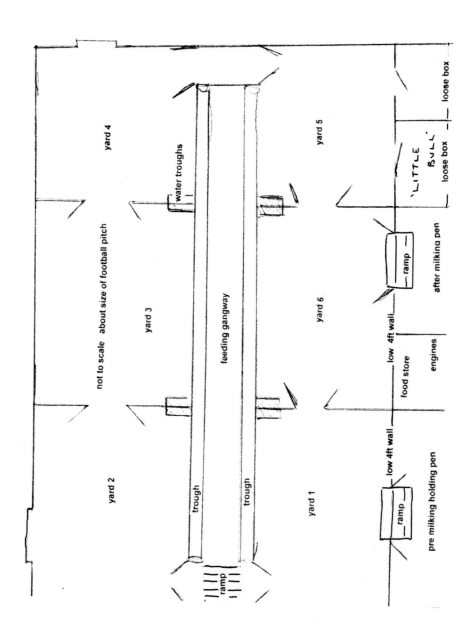

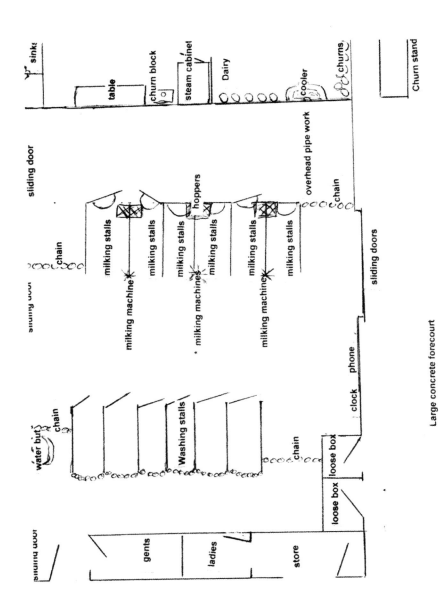

Ground plan of the yards, bale and dairy at Merrist

Chapter Five
Days Off

My day off was my treat and I loved going into Guildford as there was a shop that supplied second hand W.L.A clothing. For a few shillings one could buy cream poplin shirts that were so much smarter than the Aertex ones. I also bought extra breeches, which I took to the dry cleaners and had dyed dark brown. One pair I found, not standard issue, were gabardine and very smart. Overalls and footwear were also available and I soon built up a wardrobe of decent clothes for work and best.

On the High Street, Marks and Spencer and Woolworths had their place, as did the second hand bookshop. Oh, how I loved to browse in there. It was like wonderland to me and I made many additions to my book shelves. I bought copies of old favourites and others that I eagerly anticipated reading.

One day, on turning a corner I saw the fashion shop; you know the kind, with just one outfit tastefully displayed in the window. I stood gazing at it, a lady's costume (or suit we would say nowadays) of a lovely dark rose colour and tailored in quality material. The discreet price ticket stated 'four guineas'. I decided to do the rest of my shopping, then found myself back at the shop window again. On venturing into the plush interior, the assistant said the costume was my size, Maid's 8, and when I tried it on I felt it had been made for me. I plunged, counted out my clothing coupons and the four pounds, four shillings. With my purchase folded and wrapped in tissue paper in the shop's exclusive carrying bag, I left the shop walking on air. It was such a feeling of independence. Looking in the nearby Clarks shoe shop, I earmarked a pair of leather high heels and matching hand bag for a future shopping trip.

The Pilgrims Way follows the river Wye as it flows through Guildford; it was a pleasant stroll along the river banks. Rowing boats were for hire and it was always a source of free entertainment just to sit and watch the rowers; there were shades of *Three Men in a Boat*. Some could handle the boats while others were just trying to show off and usually got very wet.

The Forces Canteen was run by the lovely, motherly ladies of the W.V.S. who served up a good cup of tea and beans on toast at a reasonable price. The Canteen was well patronised by all the service personel, such as Welsh and the Irish Guards who were stationed at Pirbright, A.T.S. girls from Stoughton, service men from Woking and Aldershot and a few fellow Land Girls. There was always someone to have a chat with and share a table.

Another gem I found was the 'Rep'. It was a cosy theatre where a different play was performed each week They had an up-and-coming cast of actors and actresses, many of which went on to film and television. By becoming a member, I could leave my shopping in the cloakroom, enjoy the play and to top it all, you could order a tray of tea and biscuits to be brought to your seat in the interval. I got tickets for most weeks and enjoyed so many plays. All my happy memories of Guildford include the Rep.

Merrist Wood lay in a triangle of land with the Woking Road to one side. I used to alight at the New Inn, a couple of stops before Pirbright, if there was some enthusiastic guardsman offering to walk me home. I used to tell a little white lie saying that I was only going to the cottages on the Green, near the bus stop. Where I did proceed to call, but only to collect my bike, it was very handy, as the old gentleman that lived there would mind the bike, repair any punctures and check the brakes for a shilling. One day, things backfired on me as he said that a guardsman had called, asking for me.

The other side of the estate was along the Aldershot Road and my stop there was Newlands Corner. This was the scene of a mystery as Agatha Christie had abandoned her car there when she disappeared. I usually left my bike at the sheds and could not go to collect it without saying 'Goodnight' to the girls and see that all was well with them. There is something very satisfying to lean on the gate and just watch the herd. Many of the cows would be led down chewing the cud while some would amble over for a pat. Then I cycled up the lane towards the open gates and the twinkling lights that welcomed my return.

Chapter Six
Dairy Matters

Wednesday mornings brought regular visits from the vet. He not only cast his eye over the herd, but also gave lectures to the students. I did not advise volunteering to help him unload his car, as I made several grizzly finds – it was quite usual to find a cow's afterbirth slopping about in the boot, or some dead piglet or whatever else he was going to dissect to illustrate his lecture. Strangely enough, I found that on Wednesday lunch times you could get second helpings, as for some reason the students did not have much appetite!

Whenever the vet was down the sheds, I always enjoyed being involved. One morning I was standing by a cow's head while he explained the finer points of a dairy cow to the students. Later, one of the vet's own students, who had come along with him, was examining the cow. He fiddled about, taking her temperature, to which she switched her tail and gave him a look of great disdain. He whispered to me, 'What did he say was wrong with her?' I whispered back, 'I am not going to tell you'. 'Go on, I will take you to the pictures'. 'No thanks, and I am still not telling you'.

The vet knew what was going on and said, 'Come on, Audrey, what do you see is wrong with this cow?' So, my past three years of being a saleswoman surfaced. 'This is Cornflower, she is a good example of the Dairy Shorthorn breed, having a milky head, a nice straight back, and conforms to the triangular shape. She had her third calf two months ago and is milking very well, over 4% butterfat. She should easily produce over a thousand gallons this lactation. Her udder is a good shape, sound on all four quarters, teats well positioned. She is a lovely gentle cow, and as far as I can see there is nothing at all wrong with her'. I got a round of applause from the vet and the students.

The vet's lectures ranged through the alphabet from anthrax, bovine tuberculosis, bloat, drenching, calving and problems of presentation, contagious abortion, foot and mouth, the value of salt licks and mastitis. By the time we got to 'W', 'X', 'Y' and 'Z' I thought I was getting shock proof. Then from out of the dreaded car boot the vet produced a glass jar. On closer examination, it was seen to be full of big, fat, white wriggling maggots. He then proceeded to give us a lecture on 'The life cycle of the warble fly'.

Was it some fiendish conspiracy between the vet and Matron? We had sago pudding on the menu at lunch time, all white and lumpy. Even I passed on that occasion, and have never fancied sago pudding since.

At that time farmers were upgrading their herds, winter milk production was more profitable and we were working towards more cows calving over the autumn and winter so that their best yield commanded the higher price. Tuberculin Tested milk also brought a better price, so the herd was 'going T.T.'. We tested the milking herd as they came through the bale. The young stock at Cobotts Hill and Nortons farm were a very different proposition; they did not welcome being rounded up, in fact the male students seemed to regard this as a personal challenge, resembling a 'Wild West Rodeo' at times. I shook my head and left them to it. Eventually all the stock had their ear tattoos and numbers recorded, the vet then measured and recorded the thickness of the skin on the neck, then the animal had the injection. After a few days the vet returned and the whole process of measuring the skin and checking ear tattoos was performed again. Any stock that had reacted to the injection were separated. Later they were retested and if they were T.T. positive they went to market. So, we gained T.T. status for the Merrist Wood Herd, producing safe milk.

Being a T.T. herd, we fastened the lids of our churns with twine then crimped the little lead seal over the knot, using a pair of pliers embossed with our code. We also had regular visits from the Milk Marketing Board, where a lady would arrive to check all the recordings and take a sample of milk from each cow. She would come back a few days later with the results. Pat and I discussed the dairy work with her and she said that she wished all places had our high standards. Mr Hunt came up and said that he hoped she was not trying to poach his girls. Indeed, it had already been mentioned that there were openings with the Milk Marketing Board. But, neither Pat or I were interested at that time.

All little creatures are a delight and I loved our calves. When a cow gives birth for the first few days her milk is yellow, thick and rich; this is to give her calf a good start. This milk, called beastings, could not go in with the normal milk, so it was kept back for the calves. It takes a lot of patience to teach a calf to drink as they are born with a full set of teeth and a natural instinct to butt their head upwards to suckle the udder.

You have to let the calf suck your fingers, while lowering your hand into the warm milk in the bucket. Eventually, they get the hang of it and go from their beastings to normal milk and after a while Calf Gruel is gradually added. They are several months old before they are weaned. There was a small paddock where the calves went to graze and it was never a problem to get them in again. You just had to rattle a bucket and the happy little herd would scamper at your heels.

One Tuesday morning, I was asked if I would mind riding in the back of the lorry to take the bull calves to market. Previously, I had been busy in the dairy when the lorry went, so I was somewhat shocked to see the little ones tied in sacks with just heads poking out. It was a draughty ride to Guildford market, the calves were sucking my fingers and I comforted them. When we arrived the calves were lifted off the lorry and put in a pen. I asked the driver about letting them out of the sacks, but he said they had to stay as they were, or they would be all over the place. I questioned why there was not a pen with solid sides, and some straw for them. They were, after all, babies less than a week old. I wanted to go to the market office and complain, but the driver said he had to get back for breakfast. It broke my heart to leave them there, those beautiful little calves trying to struggle to their feet, stumbling and falling down again as the sack tightened around their neck. It was like some obscene sack race. Before long they would be lying in their own filth. I felt as though I had betrayed them.

When I saw Mr Hunt I told him in no uncertain way how cruel it was to treat the calves like that, he replied that he was not happy about the situation, but it was the only way the market would accept them. The vet came next morning and I told him it was a disgrace, and asked if he could do something about it. I refused to ever go on the lorry again, but my not wishing to be involved did not alter the fate of the bull calves.

When a cow calved, I was so pleased if it was a heifer, as she would be kept and reared at Merrist, but I felt such sadness to see a little bull calf, tottering, taking its first steps. I wondered on its fate. Would it be slaughtered for veal, or castrated and fattened for beef, knowing that the next Tuesday it would face the journey into market? The only thing I could do was to ensure that it had a good fill of warm milk before it went.

My heart skipped a beat whenever I saw the post had brought another letter from Bill. He had changed his signature from William, as he said he did not wish for any misunderstandings with our bull being named William, and we could hardly change the bull's name! Always witty, tender, loving and full of dreams he wanted me to share, we had such a lot in common. He had some leave due and wanted me to meet up with him in London before he went home, or better still, if I was due some time off, we could travel 'up home' together and meet one

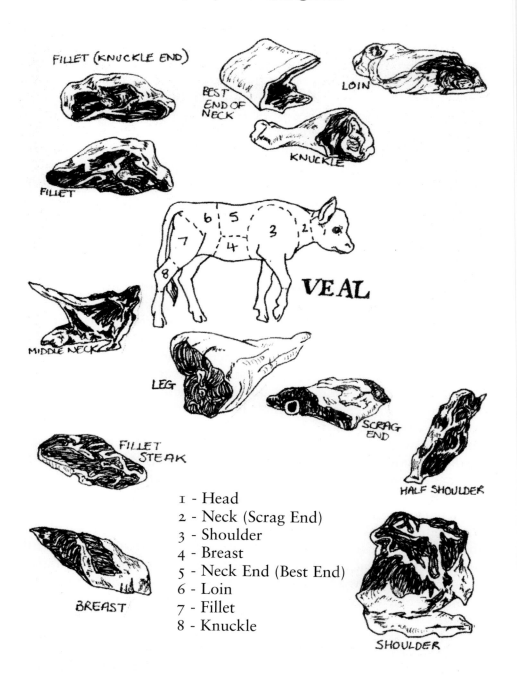

FILLET (KNUCKLE END)

BEST END OF NECK

LOIN

FILLET

KNUCKLE

MIDDLE NECK

VEAL

LEG

SCRAG END

HALF SHOULDER

FILLET STEAK

BREAST

SHOULDER

1 - Head
2 - Neck (Scrag End)
3 - Shoulder
4 - Breast
5 - Neck End (Best End)
6 - Loin
7 - Fillet
8 - Knuckle

The bull calves go to market ...

46

another's families. He even told me not to worry about getting a travel warrant as he would pay my fare.

It brought me up sharp, Bill was a man of 27, ten years older than me. After serving in the navy, six years of which had been through the War, he was wanting to make plans for his future. He could take demobilization or sign on for a further spell in the Royal Navy. He was wanting to settle down, while I on the other hand, was only just finding my own independence.

Bill wanted to come over to Guildford to see me, I was so unsure of myself and felt he could easily sweep me off my feet. Clearly recalling that evening in London, how his kisses had stirred emotions that I had never felt before, this was not flirting with lads of my own age, this was serious. I dearly wanted to see him again and yet, and yet I was fearful of where it might lead. Just that one evening together, the lovely letters, the brief phone calls, was there such a thing as love at first sight? Was this indeed love?

The author, aged 17 (spring 1947)

Chapter Seven
While the Sun Shines

The cows spent more and more time out grazing, until they only came in for milking twice a day. Tractors and trailers were brought into the big covered yards to load the dung and straw which had accumulated over the past year. The cows had tramped it down solid, some 2 to 3 feet deep. This was then taken to a field and stacked, ready to be spread on the fields during the winter.

Pat and I did the dairy, then we would spend a couple of hours helping in the fields. Here we worked alongside the other farm staff and the German Prisoners of War. We would hoe and single along our row; it was not a job I cared for, because I did not like to have to decide which little plant to leave to grow and which to chop out to wither and die. Then came haymaking; fields that had been left to grow were now mown into great swathes, we raked and turned, the air was heavy with the scent of the grass. The horses, tractors and trailers were used to cart the hay and it was made into stacks. The older farm hands could have come from the pages of any Thomas Hardy novel, they had a wealth of folklore and remembered times long gone. Bob, the thatcher, showed me how to use a pitch fork. It requires knack and balance more than strength and when Bob selected a nice medium-sized fork with sharp shiny tines for me I found that I got on well with that. Kurt, one of the prisoners, carved my initials on the handle for me. He was a young man who had been taken prisoner when he was aged 16 and he liked to practice speaking English. One day he came to the dairy to collect the milk can and from his pocket he brought out a block of scented soap, which was a luxury. Goodness knows how he obtained it.

When I understood that he wanted me to have it I shook my head as I could not accept it. Kurt looked very puzzled and said he loved me and thought I loved him, as I spoke of love whenever I gave him the milk can. Then it dawned on me; I had to explain that, as I came from

Lancashire in the north of England, it was an expression we use, to call friends 'Love'. He looked crestfallen, so I said we could be 'friends'. After that, whenever I gave him the milk can, he would say 'Thank you love'. I told him that it was not good English, but he said he liked it.

I used to lend him books; we started with *Jack London* and wended our way through my bookshelves together.

Most of the Prisoners of War were young men a long way from home. One I did not care for was older, about 35. We never knew his name, so we just called him Fritz. He marched everywhere he went and he would do an 'arms drill' with a spade or hoe; he rather gave me the creeps. I did not like the way he looked me up and down, as if undressing me with his eyes. I was thankful that he was the prisoner and not the victor. If he came to collect the milk I would only measure out the two pints allowed, but if it was one of the others I would fill the can with a drop extra.

Silage making; the 'clamp' method

The countryside shimmered under the heat of that summer, crops that were knee-high soon became waist-high. First and second crops of hay were cut, then the cows were moved onto those fields. Silage was made and the sickly sweet smell of molasses hung on the air until Bob thatched the tops of the silos and thatched the Hayricks; it was then as if a village of ricks had grown out of the land.

Over the fields and woods the call of the cuckoo echoed and then the swallows arrived. I always marvelled at the swallows in flight, they were masters of the air. But my favourite was the early bird, the skylark, for I was indeed, 'up with the lark.' What a songster he was, climbing the sky and singing his little heart out, then when he was nearly out of sight, at the top of his flight, he sang his full song before he dropped to earth and into the nest again.

A letter arrived from Mam saying that if I could arrange accommodation for her she could come for a week, I was thrilled. There was a room spare and I paid for a week's board. Mam could stay at Merrist with me. This was a big adventure for Mam as she had never been to London before. I realise now that she was quite a young woman, being thirty-nine at that time.

I had decided to wear my new pink suit to meet my Mam at Guildford station. As the train pulled in I scanned the carriages and passengers, then I saw her and waved. Mam was taken aback, she said she thought 'What a smart young lady,' but did not recognise me straight away as she was looking for a Land Girl. I took charge of the suitcase and got a taxi for us. Mam was overwhelmed when she saw Merrist and the lovely countryside, as although my letters home had described it, the reality was impressive.

Mam was an early riser and she was eager to come to join me and Pat, so we fixed her up with an overall and a pair of wellingtons. Mam told me afterwards that she was amazed how, in just a few months, I had adapted to this new life. She too loved animals and it won her heart when we went to feed the calves and I showed her how to get a new arrival to drink from the bucket. One morning the Pig Man called us over to his pens where a sow was farrowing and twelve little piglets arrived. Mam shared our working days and it was a revelation to her.

On an evening stroll, I broached the subject of Bill and the advice I got was 'not to rush into anything'. Mam reminded me that, although Dad had given his consent for me to work in the W.L.A. for two years, consent to marriage was a very different matter, particularly as it was another three and a half years before I came of age. Also they had very serious doubts about Bill being so much older than me. They had put their trust in me and expected that I would not to let them down. I suppose it was proper advice, but it was not what my heart wanted to hear.

I did get extra days off that week and we went shopping in Woking and Guildford, ending with a visit to the theatre. I remember the play was *The Ghost Train*, it was very exciting. Mam was very impressed at the arrival of the tea tray at the interval. We really thought we were living it up! The week passed all too soon and I put Mam on the train bound for London.

Merrist was something of a show place and, as it belonged to the County Council, we had regular official visits. Mr Hunt would tell us that he would be bringing a party down to see the afternoon milking. Pat and I always saw that the ladies' room was nice with a vase of wild flowers on the window sill, soap and a clean towel at the washbasin. We normally wore white milking coats, but got out clean ones for the occasion. Visits from the Womens Institute, various clubs, Young Farmers, and school trips were always popular.

I loved the children's visits. 'What are the cows' names?' 'How do you know which is which?' 'Do they bite?' We explained that, although they had thirty-two teeth they did not bite, but they could kick if they were not treated gently.

Then we started looking at the differences in the cows. Tulip, had upswept horns, the nearly white one was Snowdrop, the dark red one was called Poppy, and Laburnham had downward horns, as the Laburnham flowers hang down. If it was getting to the end of milking we used to ask if one or two would like to try using the machines; a few eager hands would shoot up, so we showed them how to pat the cow, call her by her own name, dispense the cattle cake into the trough before her, then guide the cups onto the teats. We then watched the milk pump into the jars and the needle on the scale go round to ten pounds, twenty pounds or more.

So that no one was disappointed the rest of the party went over to feed the calves. I loved waving the children off to their coach, with their teachers, hearing their happy chatter; 'Miss, I milked Primrose!' 'Miss, a baby cow was sucking my fingers!' 'I am going to be a farmer when I grow up,' or, best of all, was if a little miss announced that she 'Wanted to be a Land Girl'.

One lady visitor thanked us for the visit and said that she would never again take the bottle of milk on her doorstep for granted.

The Young Farmers' questions were far more technical, relating to the workings of the milking bale, T.T. production, feeding, calf rearing, and finally, whether I would come to the pictures! Sometimes the Young Farmers made evening visits and quiz nights were held in the common room. These were fiercely contested and great fun. One evening I was pleased to be asked to join the Merrist team – we won!

Students during 'quiet hour' in the common room at Merrist Wood Hall

Chapter Eight
Holidays and Porridge

Exams were in the air and the quiet hour of an evening seemed to extend as the students seemed to have their noses to their agricultural or horticultural grindstone. Everyone seemed to be making plans. It was something of a surprise when Pat told me she had applied to go to university in October, as she wanted to make a career in Animal Husbandry. Then there were rumblings from Leo; he wanted to give up the early mornings, six days a week. He did not like the milking bale and preferred the old ways. I was somewhat daunted when he said that he did not relish another winter in the sheds; everyone was deserting me.

It was a surprise when Mr Hunt asked me if I would like to take my holidays due while he still had some staff! So, I was off home. 'Eccles here I come!' Dad met me at London Road Station, he held me at arms' length, and said that my Mam was right, I had grown up a lot.

Everyone made a fuss of me: the neighbours; family; friends; I was asked the question everyone ever to come home on leave is asked, 'When are you going back?' I went to visit the shop where I had worked, so I wore my Land Army uniform and made my old friends laugh, relating some of my adventures whilst sharing their break in the tea room.

Several customers spotted me and we chatted and I ended up serving them. I could not tell them that 'serving' had taken on a completely new meaning to me since I had to, shall I delicately say, be bridesmaid to the cows at times. Mam and Dad made my stay enjoyable; at the weekend all the family and my friends were invited to a party, our little house overflowed and everyone made much of me.

The only cloud was that my parents were not in favour of me continuing a serious relationship with Bill. They put it to me that it was not fair to have him hanging on.

On some evenings we went to the pictures, the Regent and the Broadway, where the 'mighty Wurlitzer' organ played for a sing-a-long with the words bouncing along on the screen. The programme also included the main feature film, newsreel and cartoons.

When window shopping along Church Street, 'Estelle Modes' took my eye, so I bought a new pale blue dress with a scooped neckline, fitted waist and a lovely full skirt. Fashions were getting softer and more feminine, and hem lines were mid-calf length. I loved the new style and now it was clothing coupons that limited what I could buy.

I relished my morning lie-in, but when my Mam and Dad had gone to work I felt at a bit of a loose end as all my friends were at work too. Dad asked whether I would like to come to work with him. Next morning found us going into Manchester on the bus, booking two 'workman's return' tickets. Dad drove a big lorry that delivered to food shops around Wilmslow, Alderly Edge, Cheadle, Ashton and Altrincham. We went to the Warehouse and Dad checked his load and deliveries for the day. Dad was so proud of me as he introduced me to all the other staff; I was glad that I had opted for my uniform as I helped sheet over the lorry and climbed up into the cab. I helped Dad unload at the shops. There was such a lot of fun and banter with the shop staff, even the passing shoppers joined in: 'Hello, have we the Land Army on the job now? or 'Hey Jim, does the missus know about this?', to which Dad introduced me as his daughter. At every shop we had a tea break and Dad had a smoke and a chat. I really enjoyed being out on the road with him, so I went to work with Dad each day after that.

My stay was soon over I was once again heading south to London. It was evening when I alighted from the bus at Newlands and the cooler air was welcome after the rush and bustle of the journey. Having my suitcase to carry, I took the short cut by the field path up to the house. Either side of me the corn stood waist high; while I had been away it had ripened into gold. I plucked a few ears and the grain was pithy and sweet to the taste.

In the next field the cows were grazing. I called out, 'Hello girls,' and many lifted their head and, recognising me, ambled alongside until we reached the fence. I sat on top of the stile and took in the peaceful scene. Toby, the little black spaniel that belonged to no-one and everyone, found me there, and wagged his stumpy tail, knowing I would tease the sticky bobs and burrs off his ears for him. The evening shadows lengthened, the stag beetles and bats started to fly and turning to the house I saw a light on in our room. 'Come on Toby, let's go home'; I could not wait to show Pat my new dress.

The students were concentrating on their exams and the milking groups had finished so Leo, Pat and I managed the milking. We all worked well together so it was very hectic when it came to days off,

Toby, the black spaniel

because it just left two people to run the bale. One morning, Pat had gone home the night before as she had a university interview. I set my alarm earlier as I did not want to be late. Leo and I got the work done and the milk lorry drove away on time.

On returning for breakfast, I wondered what was the matter, as the dining room went quiet when I entered. Looking in the warming oven I said, 'Oh, have we no porridge?'. This started an uproar, with the students stamping and banging the table tops.

One of the lecturers came to me and said, 'Matron wishes to see you in her room'. Matron was one of those genteel unmarried ladies that had lost their generation of young men to the Great War. I had never been summoned to her presence before and wondered what it was all about, hoping that it was not bad news from home.

'So Miss Cross, can you tell me why you did not light the gas under the porridge this morning?' I was staggered, 'Sorry Matron, I completely forgot, Pat does that and she is away today'. I then got a lecture that I had let everybody down, and it certainly must not happen again. I told Matron that as far as I knew Pat had started lighting the gas lately as a favour to the kitchen staff and that I had not deliberately missed doing it. I also suggested that the cook could have salvaged the situation, either by cooking the porridge differently, rather than in the double pan, or by serving corn flakes instead. I suggested that I could have sent extra milk if needed, and I also questioned the safety of lighting the gas and leaving it unattended with a house full of people asleep. I then added that I did not appreciate the reception I had received in the dining room that morning. Matron's neck went a sort of puce colour and she blustered, 'Mr Hunt will deal with you'.

Doing the dairy, although I had been very polite, I pondered on the wisdom of my exchange with Matron. The dried up kipper that had been my breakfast did not sit well. Mr Hunt came in; 'I hear that I have a rebel!' He asked me to explain, nodded and said that he would deal with it. When he said, 'By the way, I will be taking my lunch in the dining room today,' I knew I had an ally.

I got the rest of the story from Miss G., the secretary. Apparently Mr Hunt asked Matron to come to his office and there he told her that Miss Cross was a respected member of his staff and that he would appreciate it if Matron would treat her as such. When Matron brought up the subject of me refusing to do the job in future, Mr Hunt said that I was quite correct and the situation should never arisen in the first place. He reminded Matron that one of her kitchen staff was officially starting work at 6 am according to his time sheets, but he was apparently starting at about 7.30 am. Having got up late and unable to prepare the porridge in time for 8 am breakfast, the cook had blamed the 'Land Girl'. I believe Matron left Mr Hunt's office looking decidedly flushed and she went straight to the kitchen. The rest of the day much clattering of pans and dishes issued forth.

I did not glory in the outcome as I would have preferred it not to have happened and I did not wish to cross Matron, or the cook. When the students asked me about it, I passed it off as 'a storm in a porridge pan'. It got round that I had stood up to Matron – walls have ears in a close community like that. A few weeks later the cook gave in his notice, 'as he was not getting up at that time in a morning'. The empty vodka bottles were cleared out of his room, we got a new cook and the food improved considerably.

Chapter Nine
Changes All Round

The harvesting started quietly at first with the whisper of Bob's scythe as he opened up the field and the tall golden corn falling in swathes as he cleared the pathway to let the reaper and binder in. Then the machinery started up, working round and round the edge of the field, throwing out the bound sheaves behind it. After a few circuits the pattern took shape as we gathered up the sheaves. Leo showed me how to interlock the heads and how to brace the butts so they would stand securely against wind or bad weather, whilst letting the air through to help dry the grain. We stacked six or eight sheaves together into stooks. I was told that the church bells had to peal three Sundays over them before they were carted. There was a wonderful spirit of comradeship; we worked in pairs collecting the sheaves and building the row upon row of stooks until they marched in long straight lines across the field. Pat and I could not work in the fields all day as we had the milking, dairy and calves to attend to. However, we managed to release Leo from the afternoon milking so that he could work with the other men. We put in what time we could, even going out after tea until about 9.30 pm. Mr Hunt said that he left it up to us girls if we wished to help, knowing that we had such an early morning start.

The fields of waving corn gave way to neat rows of stooks covering the landscape. Oats, wheat and barley were all cut. Harvesting the barley is an itchy job as the whiskers stick to your clothes, get inside your shirt and cling to your socks. It was not only barley that got inside your clothes as, once, something ran up my arm and I had to retrieve a tiny field mouse from my bra. I did have several offers of help, but declined. Pat and I did not like to see the end of the reaping, as the patch of standing corn got smaller and smaller into the middle of the field and all the rabbits retreated there until they had to bolt for it, or be caught up in the machinery.

Some rabbits got away, but a lot ended in the pot, as the young village lads chased and caught them by throwing their jackets over them. I was building a stook and a baby rabbit dashed towards me so I covered it with the sheaves. Leo was working with me and he winked at me, so we built the stook around the trembling little thing and moved on. I hoped it would be able to creep away when the night came.

Pat got the news that she had her place at university to start in October, so she would be leaving end of September. I was going to miss her very much.

The students' exams were over and most were pleased with their results, so thoughts had turned to a party to close their year at Merrist. The Common room was bedecked, with music playing and much laughter. Pat had gone down stairs and I was following. I saw Mr Hunt below in the hall talking to Matron, so I took a deep breath, and with the confidence that a new dress, fully fashioned stockings and high heeled shoes can give, I descended the big oak staircase. Mr Hunt spotted me and I knew he approved. 'Pretty dress, Audrey,' he said and Matron said, 'Yes, very becoming.' I knew that it was as near as Matron would get to offering an olive branch and I thanked her.

The next morning the exodus began, the hall was piled high with luggage and the students were packing up. After all the goodbyes, the big house fell very quiet and the students had gone. There had been times at Easter and Whitsun holidays when most of the students had gone home, but this was very different as they were all going their various ways, and would not be returning.

On the last morning Mr E., one of the lecturers, was in the bathroom when his students barged in, bagged him and shaved off half his moustache. It had taken a couple of terms to get it to its luxuriant perfection and, now heartbroken, he had to shave off the sad remains. Afterwards Pat and I tried to console him that he looked younger without it, but he had been looking forward to showing it off at home during the holidays.

A decorator was working in one of the bedrooms so I popped my head round the door to say 'Hello' and was shocked as some budding Michaelangelo had drawn a rather explicit nude, life-size picture of a girl on the ceiling. Pat said it was not her likeness, as the portrait was not wearing glasses. I said that was nothing to go by as she had taken everything else off, so why would she keep her glasses on? It must have been some male student's fantasy and it took many coats of paint to obliterate it.

There was something else that lingered, particularly in the dining room. As the days went on the niff got stronger; with the weather being warm the windows were open, but the smell got worse. Poor Toby got blamed and banned and Matron had her staff clean the room. But the odour permeated through the smell of disinfectant. Matron took to having her meals in her room. Eventually, through the buzzing of flies the source of the stink was found; a package of kippers and fish heads had been nailed to the underside of the V.I.P. table that seated Matron and the lecturers. The students had left a note attached and I was glad they had, as I did not wish to be associated with any of their farewell presents.

I wrote a letter to Bill, then tore it up and tried again, but whatever I put, or however I worded it, I had not the heart to post it. When I eventually wrote, I told him that my parents were against me being serious, especially with him being so much older and that they would not agree to any engagement, however long. In all fairness to him, I thought we had better end our relationship.

I got several letters back and a phone call, asking me to rethink and telling me that he was willing to wait. In his last letter, Bill sent me his home address in Bolton in case I changed my mind in the future. I suppose my parents were right, but somehow, something had gone out of my life. I did not dash to waylay the postman any more.

I pondered on what love is; what is that special chemistry that two people feel for one another? Why should one go weak at the knees when that person kisses you? Why did I tremble in his arms? I was so scared of my own passionate emotions that I had made an excuse that I was working when he had leave and wanted to come to Guildford. It was not Bill I did not trust, it was myself.

Chapter Ten

Seedtime and Harvest

The glorious summer went on and the corn did not stand its 'three Sundays' in the field. As soon as it was ripened and dry enough, the carting began. Every grain of that harvest was valuable; war-torn Europe needed feeding. For the first time we had our bread rationed, something that had not happened at all during the six years of war. Pat and I joined the harvesters in the fields, the sheaves of corn were pitched onto the carts and trailers until a good load was built up, then it was trundled off to where the ricks were being built.

We competed for who could lift the most sheaves at once. I could comfortably manage four together. It had to be done correctly, presenting the sheaves the right way to the loaders, butt ends out, heads inwards and the prongs of the pitch fork had to be turned over so the loaders did not catch their hands on the sharp spikes. I found that it was true that it was knack and balance, rather than strength, that mattered and it soon became natural to swing the sheaves proudly on high, to the top of the load.

Under the supervision of the older hands, the ricks took shape. A wonderful spirit of comradeship filled the fields; I think I discovered the meaning of 'all pitching in together'. The German prisoners discarded their jackets with the 'target patches' on the back, and worked, stripped to the waist, alongside us. We were young and old, men and girls, all with a common purpose; to safely gather in that great harvest.

When the end was in sight several flagons of cider arrived on the scene, we sat on the empty carts and had a sing song, passing the bottles round. We toasted the harvest, the weather and each other and we had a wonderful feeling of the satisfaction of a job well done. The last two sheaves were put aside; one for the Harvest Festival at church and the other to follow the old custom of hanging a sheaf up in the barn, to help the birds through the winter.

I received letters from Lorna; she was not happy with her posting as the farm belonged to a father and son and she was the only female in the house. During the day she kept a pitch fork handy and pushed a chest of drawers behind her bedroom door at night to be on the safe side.

The author, writing letters at dinnertime

Approaching Mr Hunt, I asked if he would he consider Lorna as replacement when Pat left? I got my reply immediately, 'She's one of Miss Dan's girls, you have worked together and been room-mates before? ... That's fine.' Writing to Lorna, I got a reply by return post.

Mr Hunt applied to the W.L.A. for her to be transferred. Lorna gave in her notice and would also be taking some holidays due, going up home to Liverpool. She could start at the beginning of October.

Several applicants for the job as Herdsman came for interviews. One morning we were told that a new man would also be starting in October.

With the new intake of students, it looked as though October was going to be a time of great change and extra responsibility for me.

Pat and I borrowed the Herd Book, and for several evenings we had our heads together, drawing up a big chart giving each cow's ear number and Herd name. I also made my own record of the calving dates and serving dates. Somehow I felt that I needed my own reference when Leo and Pat left as I was very much aware that I would be the only person to really know the cows.

Nothing stayed the same; even the cows changed as they calved and came back into the milking herd and when they were seven or eight months into gestation with their next calf, we would dry them off. They went over to Nortons farm until they were near calving again. Then they were brought down to the pens where they calved and rejoined the milking herd. This ran to a 12 to 13 month cycle, depending on when they were put to the bull.

Of course, animals have their own ideas and things do not always go to plan. Each cow was a character; take Daisy. She was dried off and taken over to Norton's Farm until she was due to calf again. The next morning she was found waiting patiently outside the sheds for the herd to come up for milking. We took her back to Norton's and could not find how she had got out. The next morning there she was, waiting at the sheds again. We gave up before she did and let her come through the Milking Bale. She was not being milked, but we gave her a small ration of cattle cake and she plodded happily on her way. Evidently she preferred the company of cows she knew, rather than those flighty heifers over at Norton's.

One morning she did not come up from pasture with the herd, so after milking I went to look for her. There she was, lay down with a lovely little heifer calf. Although the calf could walk, I picked her up and carried her up to the pens. Daisy ambled along side me. So, Daisy 4th had joined us. I was late for my breakfast, but it did not matter.

When heifers had their first calf, they needed a herd name. If they did not have one they were given one, so Marguerite, Freesia, Thrift, Thyme and so on joined the herd. When a new heifer was coming to the Bale for the first time, we tried to do it as quietly and gently as possible. How they were introduced to milking could set their pattern of behaviour and kicking cows were not welcome, so we coaxed with cattle cake until they accepted the washing and milking routine.

Pat had lectured the agricultural students last year on 'dairy hygiene and care and maintenance of the Bale'. She said that it was likely that I would be asked to do it this year, as I was now the Senior Land Girl! I helped Pat with her luggage to the taxi and wished her well as we waved goodbye. I was going to miss her, bless her. She had always been friendly and helpful to me.

Losing Pat left us temporarily short staffed, so Mr Hunt let one of the other farm staff help, feeding and littering the yards. However, Leo and I could not get any time off. Indeed, it was really too much work and would keep us both at full stretch. Ideally to run the bale you needed three or four staff to cover days off, calvings and emergencies. But we started work a little earlier, finished a little later and between us we got the job done and never failed to get the milk lorry away on time each morning.

With a mug of milk, fresh from that morning's milking and a couple of rounds of toast done over the boiler fire, I worked through my breakfast hour to get the dairy done.

It was a lovely mellow Sunday morning as I cycled to church. I passed the fields where the cows were grazing; they were a pleasing sight, sleek and content. On the other side of the lane the stubble fields were empty and shorn of their bounty. From atop of the gate post a thrush threw his song to the sky. I felt myself privileged to live and work in such surroundings. I pondered on the war we had just come through, our blitzed towns and cities, the many poor souls in prison camps, the men fighting in jungles and deserts. The Arctic seas of the Russian convoys must have dreamed of seeing a sight like this now before my eyes. England was indeed a green and pleasant land and I was grateful that we were now at peace.

At the Harvest Festival, the lovely little country church was aglow with fruit, flowers, homely jams, honey, bread and sheaves of corn. The riches of the earth flowed on to the altar steps. I slipped into a pew at the back; the church was full of people I knew and worked with. I noticed a polished milk can stood among the offerings.

Old familiar hymns lifted your heart. Ancient words took an a newness of meaning and I felt that I had truly played a part of the wonderful rhythm of country life; 'the seed time and the harvest'.

Chapter Eleven
New Friends

The lecturers and other staff returned from their holidays, ready or not for the new students. Matron was marshalling her staff, windows were open, rooms cleaned, beds made up. Then the weekend came and people were arriving. The old house was alive again and I was involved helping to welcome and direct the newcomers. By the Sunday evening nearly everyone had arrived and the common room was full of chatter and music. I went outside for a breather. The days were closing in, the mornings were misty and soon we would be keeping the cows in at night.

By the annex stood a row of motor bikes: Norton's B.S.A; Aerial; Harley Davidson; Triumph; A.J.S.; an Indian. While I was looking at the bikes I heard a familiar voice. "Hi Audrey! Which one is yours?" It was Lorna; my workmate and room mate had arrived. As she unpacked, Lorna regaled me with stories about her last place and her trip home to see her family. It was so good to have her join me.

First thing the next morning we were both off to the sheds. Lorna took to the job as I knew she would and I encouraged her to get milking – the sooner she was proficient the better. I fastened up the identification chart in the milking bale and Leo approved.

A furniture van was down the lane at the lodge; the new Herdsman and his family were arriving. The new man, Harry, was introduced to us. He was a Scotsman and seemed rather dour. Leo stayed on several days working with Harry to show him the ropes.

I was sad that Leo was moving. I knew I would see him around, but he had been good to work with. I felt honoured when he handed me his tub of Stockholm Tar – this was his 'cure-all' for cuts and infections if the cows caught themselves on wire. It was 'a bit of good stuff,' as he would say.

My eighteenth birthday brought cards and a parcel from home containing scented bath cubes, some sweets and chocolate and a sheet of clothing coupons. All very acceptable, as everything was rationed. After work Lorna and I decided to indulge ourselves. After the privations of Limpsfield, we celebrated and ran both the baths in the bathroom. Lorna soaked in one and me in the other. We luxuriated in the warm scented water and sang Land Army songs – the acoustics in the bathroom were quite good, we thought – and further indulged ourselves nibbling chocolate. Ah, this was indeed the life!

The students were getting settled in, although we did often find lost souls that needed pointing in the right direction. The Principal marched them through woods and over the fields; they covered the 600 acres 'beating the bounds'. Quite a number looked well 'beat' by the time they arrived at the sheds; they were wet and bedraggled as it was pouring down. However, they were not allowed to linger long in the shelter of the sheds. The Principal, wielding his trusty walking stick, had a purposeful look in his eye. He strode ahead and he was not going to tolerate any laggards so they were soon marshalled and on their way again. The last I saw of them, they were disappearing into the mist heading for Cobbets Hill.

The number of horticultural students had increased and were evenly split with the agricultural. Again, the intake was mostly male with only seven girls. The dining room was sorting itself out as friendships were being made.

The dining room had a little oddity; two identical doors, one of which went back to the hall. Many a one found themselves opening the wrong door and walking into a cupboard only a foot deep. This always raised a cheer, until everyone got wise that it was a cupboard for storing the billiard cues.

When I was asked about taking the students in groups to lecture them on the dairy, I asked Mr Hunt if could I have each group for a complete day – one group each week – so we could strip the bale and follow it all through practically. I did not wish to 'lecture', I wanted the students to get their hands wet and do the job under my supervision.

The day came that I took the first group. They had been down previously washing and milking, but this was to show them all the 'behind the scenes' jobs. There were six students; fortunately they were a sensible group of young men. Firstly, we set up the dairy, connected the cooler, put the cotton wool and gauze filters in the holding tank, turned the tap on, put the filters on churn and put the churn in place. I started up the electric motor, while keeping an eye on the cows, giving their names as they were being milked. I had the group also checking on the dairy, looking for how much milk was coming through – it could only run through slowly so that it was cooled properly. There could be up to 15 gallons in the system and a 10 or 12 gallon churn to receive it. Did the churn need changing?

The boiler needed lighting and stoking. We had to have steam to warm the calf milk before breakfast, so the boiler needed to be well stoked, as we needed a good head of steam to work with, on our return from breakfast.

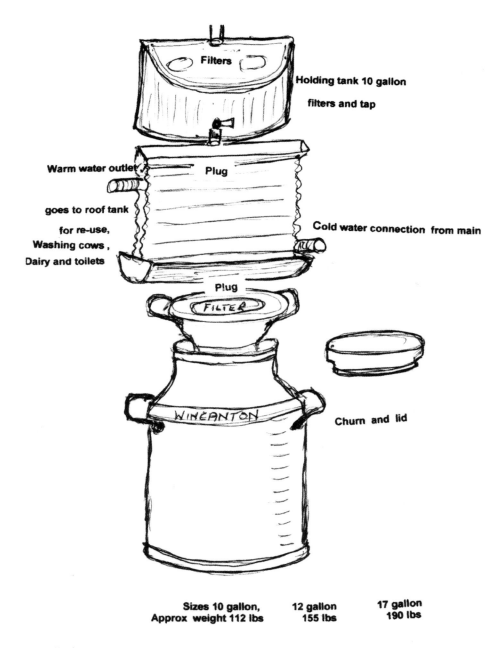

Filters

Holding tank 10 gallon

filters and tap

Warm water outlet

Plug

goes to roof tank

for re-use,

Washing cows,

Dairy and toilets

Cold water connection from main

Plug

FILTER

WINCANTON

Churn and lid

Sizes 10 gallon,   12 gallon   17 gallon
Approx weight 112 lbs   155 lbs   190 lbs

A milk dairy

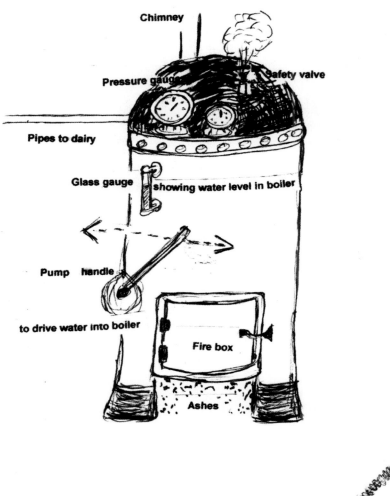

Chimney

Pressure gauge Safety valve

Pipes to dairy

Glass gauge showing water level in boiler

Pump handle

to drive water into boiler

Fire box

Ashes

Dairy boiler

Milking stool

bucket

flexible steam nozzle

A boiler

I had them measuring the churns and sealing them, then rolling them outside to the churn stand. Again, this was where knack came in; Lorna and I could get hold of the churn handles and swing it up between us onto the stand, some 3ft off the ground. The students fancied a go at that, thinking if a couple of girls could do it, so could they! A full twelve gallon churn weighs about 155lbs so you need the momentum of the liquid to help it on its way. The lads were a bit surprised, having to set the churn down again at first, until eventually they literally got into the swing of it.

We had staff milk cans to fill and needed to collect milk for the house, as well as sending the milk lorry on its way. We also had the calves to feed. I used a thermometer, as we gave the milk and gruel at 'body heat'. If the little ones were given milk that was too cool, it could give them diarrhoea (or scour).

We went back for breakfast and I asked the students to be at the dairy for 9.15 am. The boiler was sizzling like a pressure cooker. It looked like a V-2 rocket about to launch, standing some 7 foot tall in the open air with just a low wall around it. I figured that if that blew it would reach Normandy (which was a mile up the road). I showed the students the workings of pressure gauges and water valves and the handle to pump water into it. An extra advantage of the boiler was that you could do toast on the fire and jacket potatoes in the ashes. The boiler supplied plenty of hot water via a flexible tube with a steam nozzle and we did the normal dairy, scouring the cooling system, buckets and several churns – everything was stacked right into the sterilising cabinet. Then we blasted it with steam. Some of the students were making notes regarding timing, temperature, what cleaning agents we had used, and so on. Then I had the group dismantling the bale; one lad was like Tarzan swinging off the bars brandishing the spanner.

Lorna had not seen the bale stripped down before and she looked horrified: 'Do you know what you are doing? Can you get it back together?' All the very same thoughts and fears that I had when I first saw Pat doing it. I reassured Lorna, telling her 'I've done it a score of times, don't worry!' There were three milking units, so I thought I would bring in a bit of competition. I suggested that if the group split into pairs they could do a complete unit each, then if they were not assembled correctly, we knew who to blame! Mr Hunt called in to see how we were doing and gave me a wink and said, 'I see you have them all busy.'

I explained in detail how to dismantle, clean, examine, replace and reassemble. The group did well and we hung the three glass jars in place, then did the clusters. The moment of truth neared and I showed them how to fuel and start the donkey engine. The vacuum gauges flickered and with just a little tightening on a pipe joint, 'Hey Presto!', everything worked!

We steamed it through and there was now just the rest of the churns to steam on the block, then we could go for dinner. We all rolled into the dining room together and the group sat with us. We discussed many things: Bale versus Bucket machines; whether hand milking was a thing of the past; the process of T.T. testing and the merits of various breeds of cattle.

The afternoon was easier; I got them to start up the donkey engine and set up the cooler. I asked them to keep an eye on the churns as we did not want them overflowing. Towards the end of milking we fed the calves again. Then it was time to dismantle and wash all the cooler system and calf buckets, rinse the bale through and sweep and swill all the dairy and bale. That was that until next morning and I was relieved that I'd got through my first 'practical lecture'. I found it a pleasure to work with people who wanted to learn, and I too had learned a great deal from them.

The next week I took the second group. That went well, too and Mr Hunt was pleased that I had been able to step into Pat's shoes.

I found it quite odd that I was instructing students, especially as so many of them were ex service men in their mid-twenties to forties. One student who we called 'Pop' was retired and had bought a small holding. There were only a few girls in their early twenties and the remaining boys were aged eighteen upwards. I guess that I was one of the youngest – to think that less than a year ago I did not know hay from straw.

We started to keep the herd in at night which made a big change to the work, as when they were out all the time the cows only needed separating between those that had been milked and those still waiting. Now they were spread into the six separate yards. It took some observation to see if they got on with their 'pen pals'; bullying could go on and it was most noticeable at feeding time. If a cow hung back or was very timid, we moved her to another yard, until we got them settled together.

The yards had a central gangway for feeding and it was done by the barrowful. The old hands told me to position the barrow facing the right way while it was empty, then load all the weight on the front wheel. We fed the cattle mangles, kale and hay. The yards also needed a litter of straw bedding. Harry did a lot of this work while he also looked after William.

The time came to put William to a heifer. She was brought over from Nortons into the small yard near the pens. The Bull was the

Herdsman's domain – Leo had always been in charge – so I left it to Harry, but he came over to the dairy and said he could not catch the bull and asked if Lorna and me would try. Now William was a beauty, a real 'Bovine Chippendale', all 2 tons of him. We waved a handful of grass at him and William sauntered over to the rails. While he was munching the offering, we got hold of the copper ring in his nose; you had to be careful as he tried to crush your hand against the rail.

Harry clipped the six foot bull-pole onto the ring, it was our only means of controlling the animal. Backing William up into his pen, I held him on the pole while Harry went into the pen and took the pole off me, then he led William out into the yard.

Leo's approach to the animals was to let them have a good snuffle round and get acquainted before he set William to do his job. Lorna and I shepherded the heifer towards the bull but Harry rather rushed things and William was frustrated and snorting.

The heifer panicked, saw a door swing open and bolted into the end pen, hotly pursued by William. Harry tried to hang on, but he got scraped off on the door frame. He let go of the bull pole; we were in a mess, the bull could damage himself with this six foot pole swinging, attached to his nose. Also, in that confined space we did

A Dairy Shorthorn bull

not want anyone to get crushed against the wall. Even in the most dire circumstances, some humour can be found. The heifer, poor little thing, was cornered and had nowhere to go so William reared up on his hind legs to mount her and in doing so his great neck and massive shoulders lifted the supporting beam off the shed roof. The roof raised up a couple of feet in the air and Harry saw his chance, dived in and got hold of the pole and retrieved the situation. He shouted to me to 'Get under and pull her tail out of the way!' I said, 'Not likely, he looks to be doing alright from what I can see!' We backed the bull out of the wrecked pen and we were covered in flakes of whitewash, dust and straw. William strolled back into his pen; I am sure he had a big grin on his face.

Lorna and I looked at the wreckage. The pen's roof was awry, the gutter had fallen off and the door was hanging on one hinge. We dusted one another down and thought there could be a lot to be said for artificial insemination!

One morning, Mr Hunt asked me if I would like to go to the Dairy Show in London as the students were going in coaches and there was a spare seat. I accepted enthusiastically. One of the students, John, sat next to me. He had come to my notice, when on his first visit with his milking group, in the 6 am gloom, he climbed a fence and had accidentally fallen into the cesspit. Fortunately it had been emptied fairly recently, but we will not dwell on that.

It was a happy coach load; we sang and joked until we arrived. I cannot remember if it was Earl's Court or Olympia, but we were instructed to re-assemble there at 3.30 pm.

The vast Exhibition Hall was like wonderland to me. On the ground floor the cattle were on show, they were such beautiful creatures. The Channel Island breeds, dreamy eyed Jerseys and Guernseys, our own Dairy Shorthorns, Ayrshire's with the upswept horns, Red Polls, black and white Holsteins, little Kerrys, Dexter's Galloways and Highland Cattle amongst so many others. Each cow was the best example of its breed. I was interested in the demonstrations of butter and cheese making; now that was dairy work! I wondered if I might be allowed to try that at Merrist.

There was an upstairs balcony, where stalls were displaying dairy essentials. I spotted a wooden three-legged milking stool and was going to buy it and I had ideas that Kurt would carve it for me, but it would have meant carrying it round with us. John kept me company and we had our lunch together. He told me that he lived in Surrey and that during the bombing he had been evacuated to a farm in Yorkshire. I joked that he had been on the wrong side of the Pennines. He was good company and we laughed a lot.

We came to the Gasgoine milking machines and investigated them, then the Alpha Laval stand. I was in my element, as I was suggesting refinements to the design of their equipment and when asked who we were with, we said the Merrist Wood party.

Downstairs we watched the cows being milked and I remarked that if ever I had a place of my own, I would have Jerseys. John said, 'Perhaps we could have a place together.' I ignored that. Suddenly I felt like Cinderella. My watch soon showed 3.30 pm and I wished we could have stayed a lot longer; there was still so much to see, but we had to do a dash outside to find the others. We were the last people to arrive, and the driver had threatened to go without us, but he had not been able to start the coach and everyone had to give it a push. He dare not stop his engine in case he could not get it going again. It had been a lovely outing, with one regret, that I did not have time to go back for the milking stool, but it seemed that I had acquired an admirer.

The hour went back on the clocks, and I believe we were still on Double British Summer Time. We made the change in two half-hour stages, as the cows were running their milk if a full hour behind. The days were getting cooler and the ground wet, so it was decided that the cows would be kept inside all the time now. It seemed to mark the end of that lovely summer and autumn and it was with same foreboding that I faced winter, hoping it would not be as severe as the last one. The cows being indoors created a lot more work for us, as all their feed had to be barrowed in for them. One of the silos was opened and we started to feed the silage. We always fed a pen at a time, spreading the food evenly along the full length of the trough, as this gave all the cows in that pen an equal chance to feed, and cut out rivalry and bullying.

Miss G., the Secretary, called me over one day. A letter had arrived, addressed to 'The W.L.A. Dairymaid at Merrist wood'. It was from Alpha-Laval, saying they had noted with great interest the comments I had made at the Dairy Show and enquired whether I be interested in a position with their company, as they had openings in the sales and demonstration department. I knew that Mr Hunt would be aware of the letter, so I told him that I had replied and declined the offer.

Chapter Twelve
Away to the Woods

The woods had been neglected during the War, so a Woodland Management Project was started to clear and replant some areas. Strangely this coincided with the approaching bonfire night. With the help of a tractor and trailer and a gang of enthusiastic lads, before we knew it a huge bonfire some 40 foot high was built. The boffins among the students calculated as to what the mineral and chemical value of the ash would be when it was burnt.

Building the bonfire

The girls played their part making the Guy and we speculated as to who it resembled. The staff saw a distinct likeness to some of the students, but when the beard was added, a member of staff was voted favourite! We had a ceremonial lighting; it was a huge fire. We did not have many fireworks but in the last years most of us had experienced enough bangs and explosions to last our lifetime. We had cider and baked potatoes, listened to music, sang and enjoyed ourselves. The heat from the fire drove us back. I went and sat on the stile and John joined me. He slipped his arm round me and gave me a kiss. As kisses go it was quite pleasurable, but it was not like with Bill. I knew then that it would be a very long time before I could give my heart as my head told me that it was no use to get serious with anyone again until I was much older. Feeling that I had to keep things light-hearted, I joked with John that I did not know he was that observant. He was puzzled and I pointed out the hawthorn tree near the stile which had a bough of mistletoe growing on it! The bonfire, like all good bonfires lasted a long time and as we went down to morning milking, it was still a fiercely glowing heap. For days and nights afterwards the lads were prodding the ashes into life and fanning the flames (there seems to be something in the primeval memory about menfolk and fires). Eventually it rained and that was the end of our bonfire.

Lucky Guy with Freda and Phyliss

The principal with the Guy

The bonfire in full glow

Another woodland project was mooted, called 'Badgers'. It was decided to build a platform, about twenty feet up, in a tree near the badger sett, as an observation post. As badgers are nocturnal it would mean being out at night. A rota was pinned on the notice board, where students put their names down to go 'badger watching'. The platform could only accommodate two at a time. A lad called Derrick, a very shy, quiet lad, put his name down on the list and someone wrote my name next to his. It was done for a lark and no-one was more surprised than Derrick and his room mates when I said, 'Yes, I'll join you'. We headed to the woods taking a torch. Derrick climbed to the platform, and gave me a hand up. There was just about room for two and as our eyes got used to the darkness we could see some movement and hear rustlings below. We expected to see the black and white shape of a badger, but no, it just looked black. Derrick tentatively shone the torch; it was Toby. We shooed him to go home, but he was having none of it. Whatever was going on he was determined to be included.

Into the woods ...

Derrick climbed down and as we could not get rid of Toby we hauled him up aloft between us. Now there were three of us on the platform. We settled down to wait. It was surprising how much sway there is in a tree. The wind scudded the clouds along and the moon came out.

We heard voices – it was a couple and they were oblivious to us lot up the tree. Now what do you do? Keep quiet and hope they go on their way, or do you make yourselves known? The couple paused and started kissing. When the man laid his raincoat down I thought that Derrick and I were going to observe a lot more that night than the nocturnal habits of badgers. Visions of Sylvia's warnings came to mind; was this to be an above and below the waist encounter? Before things got too far, I tossed dawn a couple of pine cones to attract their attention. 'Hello, would you mind, we are badger watching,' I said. With a rather surprised squeal from the young lady, they gathered up their things and scurried off in the direction of Norton's Barn.

My silent prayers went with them that they would take all necessary precautions and close the gates! With all the disturbance I did not know if we would see any badgers. We settled down again and Toby snuggled up with us. He was getting a liking for this 'high life', especially when I produced some fluffy chocolate from my coat packet. There were more little noises from below. Peering over the edge, we saw a fox trotting along, carrying a dead rabbit for his supper. All was quiet and I was beginning to wonder if we had better call it a day, or night!

Then we heard snuffling noises and we could make out shapes below us. There were three large badgers and two smaller ones; their white masks showed up in the moonlight. One of the larger brocks kept sniffing the air as though he could scent us and we watched them for quite a while as they dug and foraged about, before disappearing down into their sett. I peered at my watch, it was 1 am. We got Toby down between us and returned to the house where the back door was unlocked, as it always was. As we went to our respective rooms, Derrick whispered that he had really enjoyed the evening and I whispered back, 'So have I.'

The next day Derrick had written up his observation of the badgers and put it on the notice board. I think there was some kudos in it for him and more than a hint of jealousy from his room mates, as they could not get any of the girls to go badger watching with them.

When ever I met Derrick out in the woods, I was happy to fall in beside him and share his binoculars. He loved nature and all wild things, he could imitate bird calls, he knew where their nests were and where the traveller's joy, scarlet pimpernel and the hidden violets, reputed to have been planted by monks, all grew. He knew the habits of the fox, hedgehogs, rabbits and squirrels, yet he was so very shy with people. I like to think that we were friends.

As the weeks went on I was coming to the end of my dairy days. There was just the last group to take. They were late down to the sheds and when they did arrive they were very half-hearted about it. I asked them to be back at the dairy for 9.15, but there was no sign of them. Harry and Lorna were over at the pens, where a cow had started to calve and we were not sure if the vet would be needed. I got cracking on the dairy and when the group did arrive, there was a lot of sniggering going on and they were passing a paper round. I was in no mood for nonsense. To get their attention I rapped my scrubbing brush on the dairy table: 'I know that you would prefer to be looking at a motor bike engine or have a tractor to take apart, but this too is farm machinery. Milking Bales are rare at the moment, but in the future you might be glad you have had this experience. We have a job to do and if we want to get back for dinner-time today, we had better start work.'

I also informed them that the other groups had all finished by noon and challenged them to better that. 'By the way, I do not know what questions will be put in your exams. There may be one or two on the milking bale, but I cannot imagine there will be any questions on "Dead eyed Dick and Eskimo Nell" so put that paper away,' I said. I was thankful the lads took it in a good spirit, one or two even looked sheepish. When they got into dismantling the bale, they worked well and we timed each pair reassembling the milking units. We finished in good time and they even filled the hoppers with cattle cake and littered the yards, jobs Harry would have done if he had not had to attend to the calving. By the end of the day, when Mr Hunt asked how it had gone, I said they just needed a push. He had a twinkle in his eye and said, 'Yes, I heard you and how do you come to know about Eskimo Nell?' To which I told him that this lot were tame compared to last years' students, as they were the ones that had left a copy of that poem pinned up in the boot room.

Chapter Thirteen
A Thousand Men and a Girl

As the weeks went on, Harry, Lorna and I got into a good routine, Mr Hunt told me that he was very pleased with Lorna and the way we worked and lived together. He told me that I could have some time off, if I would like to go home before Christmas.

I wrote to Mam and Dad letting them know that I would be coming home Friday night, sorted out my travel warrant and was ready to go! It was dismal weather a grey damp mist had hung about all day. Entrusting the care of the pulsators, the dairy and the calves to Lorna, I set off after dinner, catching the bus to Guildford. The train to London was late, people were saying that it was foggy and likely to get worse. It did and the train crawled into London. Sounds were muffled, visibility was only a few yards. The air was thick with the sulphuric fumes from traffic and thousands of chimneys and everything was wrapped in a blanket of fog.

Arriving at Euston I found all trains cancelled. I had planned on catching the tea-time train that got into Manchester about 10.15 pm, but I joined the other stranded passengers. Everyone had scarves or handkerchiefs over their noses and mouths. On making my way towards the platform that my train usually went from, I found crowds of service men, who also wanted a Manchester train. I thought about food and made my way to the Refreshment Room. It was crowded, but I managed to get a cup of tea and a couple of sandwiches, one of which I saved in my pocket. Making my way outside again, I nearly bumped into a tall, young man in naval uniform, it was a heart lurching moment; I thought it was Bill. I did not know if I was greatly relieved or bitterly disappointed that it was not him.

The Ladies' Waiting Room was less crowded, at least the fog was not as thick in there as outside. I got a seat, my mind was in a whirl, I thought myself all kinds of a fool. What would I have done if it had been Bill? If fate had thrown us back together again I know would have followed my heart.

A porter put his head in the door and announced that there would be no trains before 9 o'clock. To pass the time I glanced at an out-of-date magazine, but I had no interest in it or the dog-eared newspapers lying around. I chatted to the other ladies, they were waiting for various trains. A lady had a kiddie asleep on her knee and she asked if I could take the child and keep an eye on her suitcase while she went to the ladies' and the Refreshment Room. She came back with two teas, one for me, but said they had run out of food, so I shared my remaining sandwich with her.

About 10 pm I went to the ladies' room, the attendant was still on duty, as she said she could not get home either, and I paid my 2 pence for a 'Wash and Brush up'. In the mirror I could see my face was grimy with the fog, my nose and nostrils were black although I had used my hanky to cover over my nose. Like everyone else my eyes smarted. I was glad of the wash and felt somewhat better as I returned to the waiting room. Somewhere after midnight there was movement outside and the service men were making their way to the barrier, I asked what train it was; Manchester!

Showing my travel warrant I joined them on the platform. The men were very orderly boarding, although the train was getting packed. There was plenty of banter and quite a few hugs as I was edging my way along the corridor full of men and their kitbags. Someone got hold of my case and whisked me into an already full compartment, the lads stowed my case on the rack and made room for me to sit with them.

We asked one another where we were heading and we all came from around Manchester. It was nice to hear our own dialect and familiar place names. The men were smoking and chatting about the railway belonging to us now that it was nationalised, I did not care if it was B.R or L.M.S. as long as it was going in the right direction. The train got moving, we could not see anything out of the windows, just dark and the yellowy fog pressing against the glass. The talk, the warmth, the movement of the train ... I had been up since 5.30 the previous morning, and unable to keep my eyes open, I drifted off to sleep.

As I awoke and gradually became aware of my surroundings, I found I was leaning against the shoulder of a lance corporal. The cloth of his tunic was rough to my cheek. Stretching, I looked at my watch, and it was 3.30 am. The train had stopped and all was quiet. Looking around most of the men were asleep, we were all weary. Fog signals went off and then we started to rumble on our way again. I wondered how far we had journeyed. I knew I wanted the ladies', so I carefully picked my way over and around kitbags, packs and sleeping men all along the corridor. One compartment had a card school in progress, I was invited in to bring someone 'luck' an offer I declined. In the ladies' I had a wash again, and felt more awake and refreshed; I only lacked a cup of tea.

On returning to the compartment, Bert, my lance corporal, said he was going an a reconnaissance to see if there was a buffet car on this train. He returned with the news that there was not, and the whole train was packed with service personnel. Rummaging in my pocket I produced some Mint Imperials that I had been saving. We sat chatting; he was going home to Whitefield. Out came the photographs of his wife and kiddies. Bert pulled out his tobacco pouch, and started to roll cigarettes, neatly filling his cigarette case, he offered me the edge of the Rizla paper to lick, which was the polite way of offering me that cigarette. He was surprised that I did not smoke as most people did then.

Gradually our travelling companions woke up. I passed round my sweets, but most preferred a smoke, which caused a laugh when someone painted out that it was a 'no smoking' compartment. It was still dark outside, we had no idea how far we had come, it was agreed that as we had not stopped at any stations, the train was going straight through.

Somewhere, someone started to play a mouth organ, 'Show me the way to go home, I am tired and I want to go to bed'. We went through all the popular songs, when it got to rugby songs there were shouts up the train of 'Lady present!' By the time we got to 'My Brother Sylvest' I believe the whole train was singing. Even the engine seemed to pick up some speed, the fog was thinning, we could make out some familiar landmarks, we were coming into London Road Station.

Everyone was gathering their belongings, Bert lifted my case down, I had several offers to carry it for me, but I insisted I was fine, and they had their kitbags. I thanked everyone for their company, one or two did try to make a date, but I told them I had a boyfriend already. Walking up the platform, we passed the engine, the driver and fireman were on the footplate. Their grimy, tired faces told their own story, 'Thanks lads ,' we shouted and got a toot on the whistle in reply. As we came through the barrier, I spotted my Dad, and I felt at last I was home.

Home, sweet, home, how true those words were. To sit in the twinkling firelight, enjoying a meal and a pot of tea with Mam and Dad knowing there was a warm bed waiting for me was wonderful. Dad was full of the events that had taken place, the times he had found his way in that fog to the telephone box at the top of the road, getting through to Enquiries at London Road, to be told that there were no trains at all running from Euston.

Mam and Dad had gone to bed, getting up about 6 am. Dad had again phoned, there was one train on its way. The fog was thinning enough for the buses to start running, Dad had made his way to Manchester. While talking to the station staff they said that it was very unlikely that I could have even got aboard in London. In Dad's own words, 'I thought it was a 'troop train', crowds of service men were pouring through the barrier, I thought 'our Audrey is not on this train', then, blow me, there she was, laughing and waving goodbye to a group of soldiers. 'Do you know, I believe she was the only girl on that train.' I lost count of how often I heard that related before my leave was over.

We went visiting family, there seemed to be changes all round, my younger cousin John McAllister, was an apprentice and was growing up into a fine young man, older cousins, Edna and Alma were courting, Alma had met Eric who had been in the R.A.F. Edna was going out with Walter, a smart lad in the Paratroops, I could not help but wonder about Bill, he would have been the 'Senior Service' and I wished that I had him by my side. All my friends seemed to be pairing off too. My dear school friend, Doreen, was courting a nice young man, yet another John. I did have a family member as an escort, John Timperley. We went to the pictures together several times, we had always enjoyed one another's company.

Several days I went with Dad to work, and everywhere we called, the story of the train journey was related, of how it had taken me 14 hours from arriving at Euston to get to Manchester. A real 'pea-souper' that fog had been, Dad thought that I had only got on that train because I was in uniform and was travelling on a warrant. He may well have been right.

We had family get togethers, sing-songs, party games, then sad farewells, as I was packing my case to go back again. Mam was upset that I could not stay for Christmas, the previous year I had been at Limpsfield.

Yes, I had been in the Land Army a whole year.

Chapter Fourteen

Variety is the Spice of Life

On my return I found Christmas preparations were in full swing, a huge tree stood in the hall, the common room was bedecked with greenery and paper chains, there was great excitement in the air about a forthcoming concert. Came the night of the show, a stage had been set up at one end of the Common room, while the rest of the room was packed with students, farm staff and their families. The curtain went up on a nativity play. Lorna had told me that it had been suggested that they 'borrow' some animals, calves and piglets, but ended up dressing Toby and Ranta as a couple of sheep.

I really did not know that we had such a wealth of talent; there was a specially written pantomime which nearly brought the house (and stage) down. Somehow a rendering of Albert and the Lion, by one of the lecturers was included. We rounded off with Desmond, one of the tractor drivers, who had a fine singing voice and led us all in carols. It was a happy evening and everyone enjoyed it. The old house seemed to revel in the anticipation of Christmas.

Then once again we had the great exodus, the staff and students, even those who did not normally go home at weekends because of the distance, were travelling home for Christmas and New Year.

Lorna and I had to work over the holiday, I remember standing at the top of the staircase looking down into the dark vastness of the hall, everywhere deserted, even the Christmas tree had been taken away, there were just the echoes of the laughter and the singing.

I was glad to join Lorna in our room, it was warm and bright. Before he went home, John had cut a fir branch out of the woods for me, which we lay along the mantle piece, and we dressed it up with what trinkets and baubles we had. The smell of pine scented our room, it was a little oasis of Christmas in the shadowy darkness of the great house.

It was still a few days to Christmas, Lorna and I were alone in the house, and we got our own meals and looked after ourselves; it was then that I found Lorna was a dab hand at making flapjacks and other goodies. We quite enjoyed ourselves as we took our meals up to our room. We had our book shelves, a wireless set, a newly acquired electric fire, and it was luxury beyond compare to the harsh conditions that we had endured at Limpsfield.

Came Christmas Eve, away in the depth of the house the call-box phone was ringing, Lorna and I looked at one another, should we bother answering it? It was not likely to be for us, also it could ring off before we even got there. We both made a dash for the door, down the stairs and picked the phone up, it was Desmond, having told his mother about us being on our own, she invited us to join them Christmas Day when we had finished work. Desmond lived at Woking and had checked that there was a train through Worplesdon at about 5 pm. He would meet us at Woking station. Also there was a train back at 11 pm, would we like to come? Yes, Yes, Yes!

Lorna and I suddenly decided that we would go to the Christmas Eve Service, we wrapped up warmly for the night was bitterly cold, we rode our bikes along the lanes to church. Everywhere was like fairyland with rime thick upon the bushes and trees, over head the star filled sky. The church was aglow with candle light, we listened to the age old story of the Nativity, told in all its simple, wondrous beauty. It was a lovely service, we sang the familiar carols. At the church door a chorus of 'Merry Christmas' followed us as we mounted our bikes. During that evening I had been reading a poetry book, which included 'The Oxen' by Thomas Hardy, this raised the question, did the cattle really kneel at midnight on Christmas Eve? Well there was only one way to find out. Oh, what it is to be young!

We made a detour.

Creeping over to the yards, we looked and saw the cattle were all down in the rustling straw, whether they lay or knelt, it was hard to tell in the moonlight. The church bells were still ringing, peal after glorious peal, their joyful sound carried over the frosty air.

It was Christmas morning, the Christ child was born and I believed I had seen the cattle kneeling! 'Peace on Earth, Goodwill to all men.'

Christmas day and it snowed. Cows have to be milked and all the animals fed and cared for whatever the day. Thoughts turned to home, as I had managed to get a bottle of my Mam's favourite perfume 'Evening in Paris' for her and a box of cigarettes and the little cigars 'Wills Whiffs' for Dad. I had left them to be opened Christmas Day. Lorna and I had parcels from home to unwrap, we both missed our families, maybe Lorna even more so, as she had a younger brother and sister.

When the afternoon milking was done, we dashed back to get ready, and just made it to the station to catch the Woking train. I can only say that the family welcomed us into their home, it was full of warmth, fun, music and love. Lorna and I helped wash up, we played party games, we gathered round the piano and Desmond sang for us, lovely old ballads and war time favourites, we ended with Christmas carols.

They saw us off at the station, when we reached Worplesdon, the station staff had gone off duty, but our trusty steeds were still there awaiting us. Cycling along the deserted lanes we passed houses and cottages, many with their windows still warmly lit, where the curtains were not drawn we looked on homely scenes. I thought then that I would try to be home for next Christmas. Over the next days we had invitations to share a meal and the fireside with other farm workers and their families, when they realised that we were on our own. We even found where Toby had billeted himself, he had taken over Leos' hearth rug. I could not help but be grateful for the kindness and hospitality of so many good people.

So the New Year came in, 1948, another severe winter was upon us, fortunately, we were better prepared for it. Our room was snug and warm, there was plenty of hot water and meals. We had extra clothing and comfortable beds.

Down at the sheds we managed very well, by taking care of the pulsators and bringing in a coke brazier, so that the pipes did not freeze overnight, we kept everything working. The cattle and calves had extra bedding and when a cow calved we gave her a warm bran mash, to set her up.

Staff and students returned and everywhere was a bustle, our dining table was popular and full. John had joined us and a land girl, called Mary, who for some unknown reason was nick-named 'Phoebe' and was studying Horticulture. I often helped her copy notes, I thought then that I could get a liking for that subject too. I also copied up John's notes from the lectures the vet gave. We had Norman, who was called 'Peypes' as he kept a diary of the student life. Derrick and Lorna and me, what a motley collection, but meal times were always great fun.

Outside we had snowball fights, and the garden had an ever growing family of snowmen. We were included, as far as our jobs allowed, with the student activities. There was the 'Rambling Club', that fell on Lorna's day off, if it was raining, they 'rambled' down to the sheds, where they changed their stout boots and left the walking sticks, 'rambled' to the bus stop and Rambled off to the pictures in Guildford for the afternoon.

If excursions to The New Inn or The Cricketers were afoot we were included. I made many trips into Guildford on the pillion of a motor bike, my favourite was an Indian, it was a huge bike and the tank was decorated with a picture of an Indian Chief in a War bonnet.

Merrist Wood Hall, New Year 1948

Sometimes several of us would cycle into Guildford to go the pictures; we could leave our bikes at a local garage for sixpence each. During one performance my feet ached, so I slipped my shoes off, at the end of the film, I tentatively felt around for them, we stood for 'God save the King', then as the lights went up, I looked under my seat, no sign of my shoes, of course I knew the students had them. As I got no response to my appeal for their return, ever independent, I set off to walk with threats of waking every one of them up at 5.30 every morning! One of the students picked me up and carried me, till his mates produced my footwear. Passers by must have wondered what a Land girl was doing sitting on a doorstep while two burly young men were on their knees putting her shoes on for her.

After the fiasco of the wrecked pen, Harry decided to try another approach with William, by clearing the first yard, put the cows to be served in there, and bring the bull over to them. Walking William over to the yards was quite an outing for him, and he rather showed off, also all the rest of the cows in the yards crowded as close as they could to the rails, to get a grand-stand view of the proceedings.

They were like a 'hen party' awaiting the arrival of the 'strippergram'. With all the commotion the cows to be served would not stand. Harry passed me the bull pole saying he would not be long, he was just popping home for something, so I was left walking this great bull round, as if in a parade ring, remembering to keep his head up as Leo had told me. One of the cows was interested, and not wishing to miss the opportunity, I gave William as much freedom on the pole as I could, and he performed.

Back came Harry with a head halter, which he put onto the remaining cow, the cows were not used to halters, but Harry eventually tethered her up to the rails. I really did not think it was necessary, as with a little patience, nature took its own course. But Harry was in charge of the bull and I had to do things his way.

The other farm staff speculated as to why Harry had a halter at home, and what his domestic arrangements were, it was something I could not possibly comment on!

We were putting cows to the bull regularly now, as cows have a nine month gestation we wanted calves to be born September, October, November, for higher winter milk production. I did not mind walking William over from his pen, except that we had to pass the shed where the P.O.W.s had their meals. The German that I did not care for, Fritz, used to pass loud comments in his own language, I felt they were something rather suggestive about Lorna and me and the errand we were on. I did ask Kurt what was said but he would not tell.

It is strange how little things come together, students, being what they are, somehow the bolt had disappeared off the gents' toilet door. Towards the end of morning milking, I nearly jumped out of my skin, when blood curdling screams and shouts were coming from the gents'.

Now Geum was a gentle little cow, she was one you could trust with visitors and children. She was waiting to come through to be milked, while in the washing stalls, we did not bother putting the chain up behind her, as she liked to have a drink from the water butt. Following the noise and screams, I found Geum had wandered into the gents', there was Fritz stood on the toilet seat, clutching his trousers some where round his knees gibbering like a fool. Everybody came to see what the commotion was, Geum was not used to having toilet rolls thrown at her, I deliberately took my time getting her out of the gents'. Nobody had a straight face, although Fritz insisted it was the bull, he never lived it down that he had been frightened of a cow and a 'bit of a girl' had to rescue him. It was about that time he stopped doing arms drill and marching about. It took some translating into English and German when asked what 'a marred ha'porth' meant, as that was what I had called Fritz.

One evening I had been down to a calving, taking my wellingtons off in the boot room, there was a commotion in the adjoining shower room. The door flew open and a student (who will be nameless!) was pushed out into the boat room and the door firmly shut behind him. Poor lad, he did not have a stitch on, so I passed him my coat which

I had just taken off. He tried to cover his confusion, but Land Army coats were only three quarter length and he was a tall lad so it did not really cover his 'requirements'. He made a dash for the other door and outside. I watched fascinated, as his pale, thin legs went twinkling along the path at the side of the annex. Then he tried to climb in through an open window, I could hardly bear to look as he disappeared headfirst inside. Next morning my coat was hung up in the boot room.

At mealtimes he sat a few tables away, I only had to catch his eye and give a knowing wink, to make him blush. Which, looking back, was rather mean of me. Considering that I was an only child and had led a very sheltered life, I must say that my life in the Land Army was something of an education!

Chapter Fifteen
Simple Pleasures

The landscape was in constant change, the stubble was ploughed in, leaving fields of rich soil waiting further cultivation. The threshing began, the corn ricks disappeared, the corn into sacks, which I reckon weighed about 2 cwt each. The straw was put through the baler, carted and stacked in the barn. It took a team of about a dozen workers to man all the machinery. I was glad I was not involved with threshing, as it was a dirty, dusty, noisy, and very heavy job. When getting to the bottom of the rick, Pig man's dog was in his element as he was a champion 'ratter' and I noticed the men tied string round the legs of their trousers. During winter, maintenance jobs were done, hedging and ditching; it is a delight to see a neatly laid hedge. Fences and gates were overhauled, dung spread. There was kale to cut and mangles to cart, they were put through a giant mincer in the barn to chop them up for the cows. By the time I had turned that handle a few dozen times, I was glad to hand it over Kurt or any of the other men. We were fully occupied with the feeding, milking, dairy, calves being born and reared.

Then once again that unfailing delight in the countryside calendar, the earth seemed to draw a deep breath and the miracle of spring was with us again; snowdrops were in the woods, then the daffodils. John and I often walked in the woods and he carved our initials on a great fir tree, 'J.E.H loves A.C.', I wonder if it is still there? All men carried a pocket knife then, smoking was normal and I liked the smell of his pipe tobacco. I was very fond of John we had a lot in common, he was a very good worker and even in his free time he would come down to the sheds to help us with milking.

I had met John's parents and brother at a Merrist 'open day' and it followed that when I had time off we went together over to Cheam and spent the day with his family. They made me very welcome, his Dad and brother used to tease me and I think John's Mother liked having a girl around. Really it was a strange relationship, as we all knew that John and I were friends, but were both too young for it to go anywhere. I believe his family did approve of me, even if I did come from 'Up North'.

We would go for a walk to nearby "Nonsuch Place' an Elizabethan Manor. John had been to grammar school and he used to recite yards of poetry to me, smatterings of which still remain in my memory.

Midst the fray see, dead and dying.
Friend and foe together lying
'—like the leaves of the forest are withered and strown—
And the women of Asher are loud in their wail,
for the idols are broke in the temple of Bale'

Perhaps someday I will remember it all and what it was called, I know it was an epic!

On occasions John and I took a boat out on the Wye, it was peaceful, the river banks were over hung with willows and there were landing places. There is something very soothing about rowing, the rhythm of the oars and the lap and gurgle of the water. I used to let John row one way, then we would take an oar each to bring the boat back against the current. Life seemed full of simple pleasures ...

Chapter Sixteen
Dicing with Death

It was with eager anticipation that we watched the cattle truck unload its special passenger, he descended the ramp tentatively, he was only a youngster, being about 10 months old. What a lovely little bull, he had just had the copper ring fitted to his nose, and kept putting his tongue out and licking it. He was pedigree stock. We were to rear him on to serve the daughters of William as they would need fresh blood. Harry took charge of him and placed him in a big loose box adjoining the yards, we had a laugh one day, as we noticed the new arrival with his head through the rails, suckling one of the cows. We thought the milk production from that pen was down, and now we knew where it was going. Bless him, he was just a big baby. He liked having his curly topknot scratched and he was a very friendly addition to the growing herd. Then we noticed that he was off his food and looked out of sorts, Harry was concerned and sent for the vet, Mr Hunt. There was much debate and the diagnosis was that the poor creature had swallowed some wire. This was confirmed at the post mortem, we were all terribly upset at losing the 'little bull'. He had been Harry's charge, somehow a piece of baling wire must have broken off and not been collected when the pen was being littered with straw, or it could have been in the hay. I felt dreadful and mourned the loss of such a bonny, good natured little creature. Although I knew that I had not fed or bedded him down, I felt it reflected on our care. If it had been a dirty milk sample, or something wrong with the calves it would have been my responsibility, as it was, I just felt so sad.

We were quite used to hearing shooting from the army range at Pirbright, but this sounded much nearer. Cycling up the lane to go for breakfast, a group of local men were loading a car with shot guns, dead rabbits and a bundle of bloodied fur. I felt dreadful, but it was nothing to the shock I felt when I next strolled in the woods with John. Going up to the big fir tree, where our initials were carved, there tied to a low branch were the mutilated little bodies of our squirrels, their tails had been cut off, even the baby squirrels had been blasted out of the drays. As John led me away, he explained that the squirrels were considered vermin and the government paid a bounty of 'one shilling a tail' to encourage shooting them.

This reward amply covered the cost of the cartridges, so it was a free Sunday morning sport to some people. John said he loved me because I had a tender heart, I was learning that life is harsh, and that it is not fair. The squirrels had been so tame and trusting, I had enjoyed watching them. This awful slaughter spoilt my enjoyment of the woods and I feared for the fox and badger family.

It was about this time that I was having real trouble with my back, I had it injured at Limpsfield when the heifer caught the bottom of my back with her horn. Although I had visited the doctor then, I was told to put some 'Germaline Ointment' on it but it had never healed properly. I found riding my bike was uncomfortable and it was giving me concern.

As spring gave way to summer, the cows were let out into the fields, again the work became easier. It came round to hay making time again, instead of building the hay stacks this year, it was decided to bale the hay. Lorna and I went out to the fields to help and we got put to standing either side of the baler and threading wires through the metal dividers that separated the bales. Then the men were stacking the baled hay on the trailers and taking them off to be stored in the barn.

This went along well and the team were bringing trailers of the loose hay, drawing alongside, then the load was pitched into the top of the baler where it was rammed down and packed into bales. One of the lads driving a tractor kept driving closer and closer behind me every time he brought a load in. Of course the overhanging load tickled my back and I got hay down my neck, which he thought funny. I heard him driving in behind me again and stood a little closer into the side of the baler, but it was not just hay that swept passed me, the corner of the trailer caught me and I had nowhere to go. I was told that I screamed, as the trailer pushed me closer and closer to the revolving belt and huge drive wheel that powered the baler. Instinct made me duck down and I found myself lying underneath the great clanking shaking baler, seeing daylight I rolled towards the other side. I remember Mr Hunt's face as he got me up, and Lorna was as white as a sheet. The brake had been put on the machine, but it took many revolutions before it ground to a halt as it carried such momentum. Sitting on a bale I gathered myself together and everyone made a fuss of me. Mr Hunt asked Lorna to take me up to the house, but I said I would be alright as I was not hurt. Of course the lad on the tractor got a dressing down and I resumed my post, on condition that a couple of hay bales were lined up behind me, so that no one could drive that close to me again. I noticed that became standard practice on that side of the baler afterwards.

Leaving the dairy to answer the phone, it was the farm office up at the house as 'several cows had got out and were in the village, can we round them up?' It was Lorna's day off and she had left her bike at the sheds while she had gone an the bus, Harry was over at Cobbetts Hill with the vet looking at the stock there. So it was just me, I did not know if I would get any help in the village, as would you believe it, same people are quite frightened of cows. Kurt was working in the barn so I asked him to leave that and come with me. I got my bike and told him to use Lorna's which was a man's racing bike with drop handlebars. When I explained the mission Kurt said he could be shot if it was thought that he was escaping. So I told him not to be daft, he was with me! He got on Lorna's bike and did several circuits around me, and laughing we raced one another to the village. Sure enough there were the culprits, they were from Nortons. Several ladies had taken refuge in the Post Office, and watched the proceedings through the window, while an elderly gentleman was defending his garden, waving his walking stick at an intruder on his lawn, the Woking bus had been brought to a halt.

Kurt and I shepherded the truants back home, although one was a frisky in-calf heifer with a mind of her own (when she came into the herd I called her 'Speedwell'). We cycled back together along the dusty lane, we had both enjoyed the diversion. We put the bikes away in the loose box. Suddenly Kurt's manner changed, he became very serious, he kissed me, and he told he had lost his heart to me the first time I handed him the milk-can in the dairy, 'you gave me such a warm smile on that cold morning, please would you marry me?' We talked, he would be going back home to Germany very soon, I told him that when he was free he would see things differently and I was sure he would find someone who would love him, I only thought of him as a good friend. To let him down lighter, I agreed that he could write if he wished. After that, I went back to finish the interrupted dairy. It had been a strange sort of morning!

Chapter Seventeen
Come Up, Come Up!

At 5.30 am the white mist was thick and lay in great swathes over the fields, all this would melt away as the sun rose up and it promised to be another scorcher of a day. Lorna and I went down over the fields to collect the cows, meanwhile we knew Harry would be setting up the dairy and lighting the boiler. As we came to the pasture where we had left the cows the previous night, all seemed strangely quiet, the gate stood open and the electric fence had been switched off: 'Come up, come up' we called, but it did not bring any response, not a bellow or a moo, or any sign of the beasts lumbering towards us through the mist. Lorna and I did not know what to make of it, we went round the field, following the hedge. But no sign of the herd, now sometimes you can miscount and leave an odd one to follow up behind, but 74 cows took some mislaying. We wondered if Harry had made an early start and had already taken the herd up for milking, Yes! that is what must have happened and the gate was open and the electric fence switched off. We made our way through the fields, back to the sheds, I started to feel uneasy though as there were no signs that the herd had recently passed that way, no fresh cow pats and some gates were closed. The milking bale was ominously quiet, the herd was not there. Harry looked at us in total disbelief when we said that we could not find the cows. In one of his rare moments of jest, Harry said that he knew the 'Didikies' (travellers) were camped in the lay by, an odd chicken or rabbit might disappear, but the whole herd of cows?

The three of us set off down the fields again in search of the herd, and yes the electric fence had been turned off. We followed the wire around the perimeter of the field, till we found where the fence had been brought down, this led into the next field, across that and into the field beyond. We called 'Come up, come up' but still just the whitewall of mist and silence confronted us. Then it dawned on us the next field had a standing crop of peas and oats nearly ready for harvesting.

Half hoping and half dreading we approached. 'Come up, come up,' we called and answering moos and rustlings were heard, as one after another the cows slowly emerged through the mist. We counted up to 70 and Harry told us to take them up and get started on the milking, while he looked for the stragglers. We had to keep the cows in till after breakfast while the men went to secure the fence. Mr Hunt and Harry inspected the field of peas and oats, it was not as bad as feared, as the crop was to be cut to make silage for winter feed. Some of it was badly flattened, but it could have been much worse, the cows could have got 'bloat' as they gorged themselves, but they suffered no ill effects beyond having the runs and our wellingtons were decidedly green for several days. We never knew who had turned off the fence and left the gates open, maybe it was the travellers wandering about that night.

There were many comments about us losing a herd of cows, one wag suggested they could have turned up at Whitby, like Agatha Christie.

Lorna arranged for her parents and brother and sister to came to Merrist for a visit, they were a lovely family and we all enjoyed their stay. I worked my day off, so that Lorna could spend more time with them.

Merrist, Summer 1948.
The Jackson family

Merrist, Summer 1948.
Lorna, with her sister, Audrey
and dog, Ranta

A lot of my opinions and ideas were being formed at that time, being an only child, I realized I had missed a lot, I resolved that if I were to marry and be blessed with children I would like to have several.

Britain was hosting the Olympic games, we were the only country willing to try to hold the first Games after the war. In the true spirit of the Games, we rallied round and brought the nations together in sportsmanship. Local 'Cross country' and 'Harriers' clubs were carrying the Olympic torch in relays to Wembley. There was a change over point at the Worplesdon Post Office, so we went up to line the road and give the runners a cheer. I remember a tall, lean, lad, in white shorts and vest bearing the Torch on high. It flared and shone with a brilliant flame, (perhaps fuelled with magnesium, I only remember seeing incendiary bombs giving off light of that intensity). We applauded and cheered the accompanying runners and Torch Bearer, as they disappeared along the road to Guildford we returned to work. We all had the hope in our hearts that it was heralding a more peaceful world, for us and future generations to grow up in.

It was a glorious week that my Mam and Dad came to visit, my young cousin May Timperley came too. She still fondly remembers Merrist and riding on a tractor, the animals and the day we went to the seaside.

May with her Auntie Bella, my Mam

Littlehampton – May, the author and friend

That was on my day off, so I booked seats on a coach to Littlehampton, it was a lovely drive through the summer countryside. Arundel Castle came into view and it was a splendid sight. We spent the day at Littlehampton, May had a donkey ride, and we all went for a sail. The captain of the little vessel told how his boat had been to Dunkirk and showed where bomb damage had been repaired. We had a lovely day and even had a paddle in the English Channel! The week went all too soon, when it came to seeing them off at Guildford, I felt strangely sad, and wished to be going back with them. I was filled with a great longing to go home again.

I learned another lesson in life, that nothing stays the same, there is constant change, not always for the better. Several men were around the house measuring and making notes, I knew it did not bode well when I found one in our room. The outcome was a plan to extend the house with another wing, to put in an upper floor above the lofty Common Room, and to use our room to accommodate more female students. We would be moved to a self contained 'bed sitter' to be converted over in the old stable block.

This was something of a bomb shell to Lorna and I, so we discussed it with Mr Hunt. One of our main problems would be meals, to be working all day, then having to get our own meals, was not very practical. Ideas were mooted with Matron that we could have main meals at the house. We found it all very unsettling although Mr Hunt said it would take some time for these plans to come about.

The students were doing exams and another academic year was drawing to its close. So exams came and went, again most were pleased with their results. Once again there was the Farewell party for the students, to which Lorna and I were welcomed. The music, the games, the fun, then the next day, the goodbyes, everyone going their separate ways. John stayed on a few days, as long as he could, coming down to help us with the milking. He was applying for jobs and wanted to find something around Surrey.

Then Lorna and I were on our own again, she was a lovely friend and workmate, she used to reckon that we needed 8 hours sleep a night. So if we had a 'late night' we had to get to bed early the next one to make up. Many a time we would go to our beds about 8.30 – 9 pm and read for a while then 'goodnight' as we had to be up so early in the morning It was not a bad arrangement.

The wonder of harvest time came round, again the crops were bountiful, the ears of corn heavy laden. The cattle were sleek and contented, the herd was growing in number. I was very proud of the calves we had reared. Really I should have been well satisfied but there was one thing worrying me. I discussed it with Lorna, she said that she wanted to go to college and would not stay beyond next year herself, there were the Christmas times that I had missed with the family. My back was so sore and I felt unsure of my health. Some instinct made me want to get nearer to home. I wrote a letter to the W. L. A. asking if there was a posting, perhaps Cheshire or Lancashire. The reply I got was that my request would be put on file.

September came with lovely, misty, mellow days, Merrist was preparing for a new intake of students, and a letter arrived for me. A posting to a dairy farm with a milk round, at Leyland in Lancashire, was I interested? Looking at a map, I could see that I could get home on week-ends or days off, so it sounded suitable. It was not without a lot of heart searching that I made my decision.

Telling Mr Hunt was very difficult as he had been a good ally to me and treated me very fairly. I had great respect for him and I knew he respected Lorna and I and the job we did. He accepted my notice and offered references, adding that he would be pleased to have me back any time.

I had gathered such a lot of belongings, especially books, that I was wondering how to get them home, till I found an abandoned tea chest and used that to pack my things. I had my travel warrant and arranged for the railway carriers to collect my box and bike.

It was with very mixed feelings that I left Merrist Wood, I had seen birth, death, the constant changing of the seasons, I had made friends and had partings, the herd and all the calves I would miss, I wondered would they miss me? I hoped the new Land Girl would be kind to them and that she would get along with Lorna.

I only had my case to take to the train, but I also carried with me memories that have stayed with me all my life.

The author joins the students at pig judging, Goxtrode Farm, 1948

Chapter Eighteen

Chickens and Spots

I was instructed to report to Fox Farm, Leyland, ready for work without the formality of an interview. Alighting at the station I found the bus to the 'Seven Stars'. As we left the town behind, the land was flat with neat hawthorn hedges. So different to the rolling North Downs and 'The Hog's Back' that had been the sky line in Surrey. Dotted about were substantial square brick houses under grey slate rooves and fellow passengers told me when I had reached my stop. It was late afternoon as I shouldered my kit bag and walked up the drive way.

Children were playing on their bikes, from the buildings came the clatter of buckets and the lowing of cows. Approaching a well-used back door, a pig put his snout over the wall of his nearby sty and grunted a greeting. The children took me into the big kitchen, and there I met the farmer's wife, Dee, cooking the evening meal. She was a bonny young woman and she showed me up to my bedroom. The children dashed off to tell Dad that the Land Girl was here.

At meal time I met my new employer and his family, as we sat round the big kitchen table. Matt, Dee and the three youngsters, the oldest a girl of about 10 and two little boys. It was then I saw, literally, another slice of family life. A large plate of bread and butter was passed around the table, the rivalry between the boys was unbelievable, as to who got the round end and who got the much prized square end, I quite happily settled for unwanted round ends. The boys seemed relieved that I was not going to be in competition for the square ends and I felt I was being accepted.

After tea Matt chatted with me about the farm, his 30 'assorted' milkers, calves, a bull, two horses, the pig, and his new investment the brand new 'hen battery'. He also had two milk delivery rounds.

I explained that I could hand milk and had worked with an Alpha Laval milking bale, Matt seemed quite impressed, he machine milked with the Gascoine bucket method. When he told me not to worry about the job, that I would soon pick it up, I felt I had heard that somewhere before.

Having unpacked my things, written a letter home, set my alarm and got into bed, I let out a yell as something furry was down between the sheets, I could hear giggles from across the landing and it wasn't the children. Investigating, I found a prickly hair brush in my bed. So this was how it was going to be. I had left my bed room door slightly ajar to get a little light from the landing so I propped the brush on top of door. I snuggled down and would see what the morning would bring. At 6 am, I was already awake, when Matt came to knock on my door and got the brush on his head. Score, one all. It seemed I had landed in the midst of a happy family and right away I was made to feel one of them.

Outside in the sheds, I soon got familiar with the milking machines, they connected to an over head vacuum line and the units were moved from cow to cow, Matt carried the full machine buckets across to the dairy. There appeared to be no record kept of what the cows yielded, indeed we got along happily without the hindrance of paper work.

As I worked my way along the row of cows Matt appeared with a milking bucket and stool, he proceeded to follow me, stripping out the cows. He pushed his cap on the back of his head and asked what I was doing as there was nothing to strip, I explained that I had been trained to milk the cows out fully on the machines, this left Matt a bit non-plussed and he checked all the cows that I had milked and seemed satisfied.

Breakfast in the farm kitchen was porridge and bacon butties for everyone. I made sure I took round ends of the loaves. I fell for the joke sugar spoon with a hole in it, and the lads, including Matt thought it hilarious. 2-1 to them.

I asked about the dairy, and I was told that was done after dinner. A young man called Robert was coming in, he did the feeding, mucking out and attended to the Hen Battery. I was to go out to 'learn the milk rounds.' We loaded up 'the van' with crates of full milk bottles and some milk in churns. I was rather apprehensive at getting into the van; the passenger door did not close properly, it had no back doors on, no glass in the windows, but on the positive side, it did have a windscreen. We lurched off down the drive onto the main road. When we got to houses Matt would say 2 pints over there or collect the jug off the step and measure 3 gills. I found that it did help to have no doors on the back, as it was easier to serve to milk from there and ride sitting on the back with my legs dangling down. We went all round the houses and Matt seemed to know what milk his customers had without any apparent reference to a round book.

Returning mid-morning there were some dogs running loose in the road, and it dawned on me then that there was no horn as Matt reached out through the unglazed window and beat his fist on the door panel, with shouts of 'clear off'. I was also having doubts as to what braking power we had. I did decline Matt's offer to let me have a go at driving.

Back at the farm we unloaded the empties and reloaded. We had a quick cup of tea then we were off again, this time heading in the opposite direction into the town. I was starting to get a liking for this job, as people came out to have a chat with us and everyone was friendly.

We pulled up outside a cafe and Matt took their crate of milk inside. He signalled me to follow as this apparently was a regular stopping off place for yet another cup of tea where Matt met up with his cronies. I was the main subject of talk, Matt telling them that I stripped out all the cows on the machines. It seemed that they decided the Land Army had sent him a 'handy lass'. I got nods of approval and on leaving they touched their caps to me. I felt I had been accepted. We finished the round then drove back for dinner again unloading the empties.

It was afternoon when I first came face to face with the dairy. It was a simple cooling system that delivered the milk into churns. There was a bottling machine, and a large walk-in fridge. All this was tiled and was quite reasonable, and through a doorway we came to what should have been the dairy proper where everything was washed and sterilised. There was a rusty boiler that looked as though it had been many a long day since that had raised a puff of steam, and the sterilising cabinet was used as a store cupboard. There where two large galvanised sinks below a window, festooned with cobwebs and a window ledge decorated with a row of milk bottles that must have been hard to wash at sometime and had been left to soak. It could not have been a bigger contrast to my dairy at Merrist, and Matt must have seen how appalled I was. I asked about the boiler and he told me it took too much fuel and they just got hot water from the kitchen to wash the dairy things. It was his farm and he was the boss, so I would have to do things his way. The sinks only had a cold water tap so I got buckets of hot water from the kitchen. I filled one sink with good hot soapy water, and the other one for rinsing. Being aware that I had to partake of the milk that came through the dairy I put a bit of elbow grease into the job, as I would not like to serve people with milk I did not fancy myself.

Soon things started to shape up and I got the hang of the bottle washing machine. When I had done all the dairy, set up the cooler and filled the crates with clean bottles, and turned them upside down to drain, I used the remaining water to clean the window, and even had a go at the row of festering bottles, the newly discovered penicillin could have been produced from the contents. I was surprised how I eventually got them clean. Then I was called for a brew before we did the afternoon milking. Robert brought the cows up from some far off field and we soon had the milking done. Matt showed me how to use the bottling machine, which worked on a sort of see-saw. You placed two empty bottles an the stand, press the lever and they were lifted up and each filled with a measured pint. Two more bottles were put on the other arm, so it filled up two at a time. The children came home from school and came to help by putting the cardboard tops on the full bottles, it took 24 bottles to a crate.

Farms had their own bottles. Matt's were lettered in red, when they were full of milk the red looked good against the white background, the full crates were then stacked in the fridge ready for the next morning's delivery. I quite liked bottling up with the children's help and their happy chatter.

Next morning brought a change in the milk round, we were going to take the horse and float, this was a high two wheeled cart, which you entered up a step at the back. Matt brought the horse, a big bold chestnut, with a light coloured mane and tail. I had never worked with horses, at Merrist I had just given them a pat and admired them, but now I was confronted with an armful of harness, the float and 'Prince'. Matt just told me what to do; 'put the collar over his head', I found that it had to be put on upside down over his face then turned over on his neck so that it fitted comfortably.

'Right, back him into the shafts' and so on, until I had harnessed the horse. Matt checked over what I had done and nodded. We loaded the float with milk churns, measures, and full crates of milk. Matt told me to 'Hop up' and he gathered up the reins, a quick 'walk on' and Prince threw his weight into the collar and we were off.

Doing the round with Prince was a very different experience to the van, housewives came out to collect their milk bringing an odd crust for the horse, children were lifted up to pat him, in fact Prince was a star, and he knew it. When we had done both the rounds and were on the long straight road home, Matt handed me the reins. I stood up at the front of the float, it was wonderful to feel the horse respond, we went along at a spanking trot. A van started to overtake, I just held our speed and for a way he drove along side, it was another farmer and he waved and shouted to Matt, 'has she got a boy friend? We could do with getting my lad married off.'

Back at the farm the float was unloaded and backed under the shed, Prince was unharnessed, I turned him out into his field and watched as he rolled on the grass, then he trotted over to me and I patted him, I knew I had made a new and loyal friend.

The post brought several letters and cards for my nineteenth birthday. Mam and Dad had sent them on for me, one from Lorna with the news from Merrist, she missed me very much, my replacement practised the violin, (not very well). Also Lorna had started doing the 'Dairy Day' with the new students. I had a letter from Kurt, he was adjusting to life back home and had got extra work as an interpreter. The boys saw the German stamp and wanted it, and not wishing to favour anyone, I said I would keep it till I got another letter, then they could have a stamp each.

There were several letters from John, he had given in his notice at the job in Surrey as he wanted to be nearer me. His last letter was addressed to Leyland saying that he was on his way north as he had taken a job as cowman at a farm near Nether Alderly in Cheshire.

I quite liked doing the milk rounds, it came to the weekend when we collected the money. Still no sign of a round book, but we went delivering, the customers paid their bills; they knew how much it was and so did Matt. When we got to the second round, Matt put some change in my jacket pocket and I dealt with the customers, instead of having to go back and forth to him for change, I just reported to him who had paid and how much.

When we got back for dinner we emptied my pocket out onto the kitchen table, this method of book keeping seemed a quite satisfactory arrangement for Matt. I knew that I had emptied my jacket pocket, but later I found a £1 note in there, on finding it I said to Matt 'here, we must have missed this, it will be yours, because I carried no money of my own.' I knew he was testing my honesty, if I had said nothing and just kept it, he would have known that I was untrustworthy. He must have thought it well worth risking a £1 bet on me.

He seemed to run his business on good will and mutual trust. Customers out at work would leave their milk money under stones or in a bottle. In one case I never met my customer. I went round to the back door, which was on the latch, and on the table would be a milk jug, which I had to proceed to wash, measure out the milk and put the fresh milk in the clean jug into the pantry, and carefully cover it with a circle of net with a beaded border, to keep dust or flies off. The milk money was left on the table, as was the book and money for the insurance man, window cleaner and newspaper boy. What trusting times we lived in.

Chapter Nineteen
A Gentle Giant

Within a week I had cleaned the dairy, making armies of spiders homeless, some big ones waving eight white socks abseiled past me down the walls as I wielded my white-wash brush. The place took on a fresher air and I scoured the sterilising cabinet and used it for storing the washed equipment. I cleaned out the boiler, given time I bet I would have that going again. At my request, Matt fixed me up with a strip cup, a couple of new buckets, some 'Deosan' dairy disinfectant, and cloths. I had explained the routine I had been taught at Merrist and he was quite willing to give it a try. I washed the cows udders with warm water, as I explained I thought it helped the cows 'let their milk down' as well as cleaning them.

I used the strip cup to check there were no signs of mastitis, before the cow was put on the machine. When the cow had given most of her milk, a gentle stroking downward of the udder would strip her out. The milking cups were dunked in the bucket of mild disinfectant between each cow. Matt said he was impressed, as it stopped any infection being spread from one cow to another. The little extra time it took was compensated for by not having to follow the machine's hand stripping, as I showed him, the machine would do the complete job if used properly. My biggest sense of achievement was when I saw Matt and Robert doing milking the same way I did.

One morning Matt was going to a sale and asked if I could do the rounds with Prince. Dee said she would come with me if I could not manage it. I confidently said I would be alright, but I must admit that I did have qualms when it came to it. As I harnessed Prince, I had a very serious chat with him, explaining that I was a learner and that I hoped he would look after me. I am sure he understood every word, as he gave me such reassuring nods snorts and neighs.

Standing up at the front of the float, I felt like Boadicea in her chariot, a great sense of companionship with the horse came over me,

I handled the reigns gently, but firmly and he responded readily. When it came to delivering milk I had to leave the float, I stopped putting the brake on, as Prince would amble along to the next delivery. Blow me, the horse knew the round better than I did! As we clattered back into the yard after the first round I felt we had a good partnership. Going out on the second round was a little more tricky, as out of the drive we had to make a right turn across the main road. I did wonder whether to dismount and lead Prince across, but no! I think that would have been an indignity for him, we waited till all was clear and as soon as I gave him the signal we were off. (I think the horse looked both ways too).

As we finished that round, we had the long straight road home, I let Prince have his head, and he set a good pace, all the empty churns and bottles rattling around me, cars tooted as they passed us and people gave us a wave. We bowled into the yard in good style, Dee was there and said, 'you have a visitor' and there was John. Oh! it was such a surprise to see him again and be held in his loving arms after weeks apart. We had so much to talk about. Matt let me finish early, John and I caught the bus into town and we spent some time in the cafe before John had to go for the train to Manchester. It seemed to set the pattern, as in the coming months we seemed to spend so much time seeing one another off at bus or train stations.

There was another character in my life, the pig, a large white, he lived in the sty near the back door, when ever I passed I always had a talk with him and he stood up with his trotters on the low wall for me to scratch his head and back. I called him 'Fred' and was quite fond of him. Matt reckoned that I thought more about that pig than my boyfriend, well I certainly saw more of the pig! It became my job to feed Fred, his tail was always curly which showed he was happy and healthy. Fred was a clean, very friendly pig, as intelligent as any dog.

John and I arranged that we had our days off together and we met in Manchester or at my home in Eccles, it was two buses and a train for me and two buses for John. Mam and Dad had already met John at Merrist and it worked out quite well. I was concerned that John's job had no real prospects; I was sorry that he had taken it just to be nearer me. I did not want his parents to think he was wasting his time and education on my behalf. Others from Merrist had got jobs as Farm Managers or working for Agricultural suppliers. He often talked of his ambition to buy or rent his own farm; and he was saving hard to try to get some capital together.

But on a lighter note, my Dad found a joke shop and supplied me with some ammunition, one good one was imitation 'blue bottle flies'. I tried one on the tea table, Matt rolled up his newspaper to swat it

Fred the pig

before they realised it was not real. We wended our way through ink blots, dog dirt, this was very realistic on the back of the toilet seat. When it got to the boys and stink bombs Dee called it off saying we were all 'a load of big kids as bad as one another'.

Household goods were in short supply and Matt got word that the local store had a delivery of washing machines. Matt told me not to say anything to Dee, as he bought one and arranged delivery.

At our usual stop in the cafe, Matt was doing a deal with one of his farming friends, the up shot being that we all set off on a detour to look at a Friesian cow. I sat in the van until I was invited to have a look at her. I felt quite honoured to be included, she was a big, good looking cow, but I did not wish to praise her too much as the deal had not yet been done. Eventually the two men spat on their palms and shook hands at £80. We continued on the milk round and Matt was pleased as punch, and I agreed with him that he had got a very good looking cow, but again I was told not to say anything to Dee.

At dinner time I felt something of a 'gooseberry' as Matt was sweet talking Dee, saying he had a surprise for her, just to show how much he loved and appreciated her. Sadly the delivery arrangements did not quite go to plan, as a truck drove into the yard and started to unload the cow. Dee's face was like thunder, she just stood in the kitchen doorway arms folded, it is a pose that North Country women have in bred.

The situation was made worse by Matt being very attentive to the cow, patting her and walking her over to the byre, installing her and giving her feed. Robert was also admiring the new addition to the herd and I thought I had better get on with the dairy and keep out of the way. Later Matt came over to the house, and asked Dee what name they should give the cow. There were raised voices, a few choice names were suggested – poor Matt was getting a real telling off. The next delivery van arrived and I sent the men to the kitchen door. What a transformation; 'a washing machine! For me? Oh, Matt!' All was forgiven.

It was decided to house the washer in the big lean-to shed that came to the back door, the services of a plumber were needed. In fact he put hot and cold taps for the washer, installed a hot water tap in the dairy for me and a flush toilet outside in place of the earth closet. We were really getting modernised. It was a special day when the washer was first filled and loaded with soap powder and clothes. It paddled away merrily, it was a deluxe model and had a wringing machine with rubber rollers. Dee was in her element, she was washing when we went on the milk round and was still going strong at tea time. Everywhere was festooned with lines of washing. Then there was the 'ironing', huge mountains of it, Dee needed a hand to fold bedding and sheets, curtains and endless piles of clothes. Poor Dee, she had got so carried away and I had to help out with the ironing, if I wanted curtains to my bedroom window that night.

The name of Leyland was renowned world wide for the manufacture of trucks and buses, my last deliveries were on a road that led to 'the works'. I liked to be clear of there before the lunch time buzzer sounded, as a great stream of workers would pour out of the gates, it was like going against the tide. If I had done the deliveries and was turned round I was then going with the great flow of people. This enhanced my fancy about Boadecia, standing tall in the float, above the sea of bobbing heads, leading my boiler suited army. Prince also got ideas above his station, as when the buzzer sounded, it was like a bugle call to him, a war horse going into battle could not have pricked his ears more sharply, carried his head more proudly or lifted his hooves more smartly; he fairly pranced. I got a lot of teasing off the workmen and chat from the apprentices, they were a good natured lot.

My first visit to the hen battery was a shock, the din of hens clucking and cackling greeted me, then the sight of hundreds of little brown hens in row upon row of wire cages, it seemed obscene to keep any creatures so confined. The lights came on by a timer early morning and went off about 9 pm evening to keep them feeding and laying. I told Matt it was like a concentration camp for hens, but he explained that to produce the food and make a living, these methods would have to be used. Soon most eggs would be produced in this manner. I did note that there were cards to record which hens laid. If the cards on the cages near the doorway were to be believed, those hens were not laying. Matt was looking at them and said they were not worth keeping. I did point out that when people came for eggs they would take the first they came to and perhaps did not record them on the cards, so the poor hens were not getting any credit for what they had done. Matt said he noticed I always stuck up for the animals. Maybe I saved their necks, perhaps a little life in the battery was better than no life at all. Scores of generations of hens have been subjected to the battery system, I thought it a disgrace nearly sixty years ago and I still do.

The cows went to some fields the other side of 'The Seven Stars' and at times it fell to me to fetch them. The bus came along about 3.15 pm just as the cows were coming over the junction and down Fox Lane, if the bus was near I held the cows back, but if it was not in sight, we meandered along. Although the dog came with me, I could not command him, as he only obeyed Matt's whistles. I had to keep the cows from browsing as they passed the gardens, as any complaints Matt usually allowed something off their milk bill to pacify the neighbours.

If I got in front of the bus, the driver used to fume, revving his engine, and passengers shouted out of the windows, but like a convoy of ships, we could only go at the pace of the slowest, and Dolly Daydream was always last.

As the days drew in the cows were indoors at night and only went out for a few hours in the day if the ground was firm. Prince and his stable mate Duke, a big cart horse, were in at night too. I enjoyed going out after tea to groom them with the dandy brush, I used to talk to them, it seemed the most natural thing to do and I would slip them an apple or a carrot before I said 'Good night.'

It had been a nice weekend, John had stayed at home with me, we had been to the pictures and out and about together. Sunday evening we had our parting, he put me on the train for Leyland, then went to get his bus.

Monday morning I noticed Fred was not in his sty. I asked Matt where he was, and was told 'in the kitchen.' Knowing what a tease Matt was, I guessed this was another joke coming on. Dee was in the big scullery adjoining the kitchen, on the slab she had a leg of pork and was rubbing it with salt, I felt sick as I looked in a big basket, there were joints and pieces of a pig. Dee said that the butcher had 'seen to' Fred while I was out of the way. What could I say? I knew I could not eat any of the meat. I did help Dee rub salt into the hams and wrap them in muslin, it seemed strange to be rubbing Fred's cold dead flesh, when I had so often scratched his happy, warm body and pulled his curly tail. I had tears rolling down, till Matt came in and said that the meat would be too salty if I cried all over it.

I had no heart to eat Fred. It is all well and good to be vegetarian, but when you are hungry on a cold morning, I consoled myself that we were still eating rashers from their previous unknown pig, and oh! they were tasty with an egg, the best dip bread in the world and brown sauce.

Matt had some tickets to a play the local players were performing, 'When We are Married" by J.B.Priestley, it is an excellent northern comedy, I was happy be invited to go with them. I decided to have a change from trousers and wore my favourite blue dress. The hall was full and I knew many of the people, as they were our customers. I spotted Dave, the farmer's son that drove their van, he always tooted and waved, now he was making a bee line for us. Exchanging pleasantries with Dee and Matt he asked if he could sit next to me. I rather felt there was some manoeuvring going on. The lights went down and the curtain went up, I love the theatre and missed the Guildford Rep, I really enjoyed the play, the company and the box of chocolates Dave gave me, (a whole month's sweet ration), which I passed round and saved some for the children.

However, I did become aware as to how sore my back was, when it came to sitting on the seat for a while. As Dave helped me on with my coat, he said he enjoyed the play and perhaps we could do it again. He used to drop in the cafe when we were there. When he started asking me for a date, I told him that I had a boyfriend but that did not stop him meeting me in the cafe, or driving behind, or alongside on the road home. Strangely enough he called me 'his Boadicea' – I can't think why!

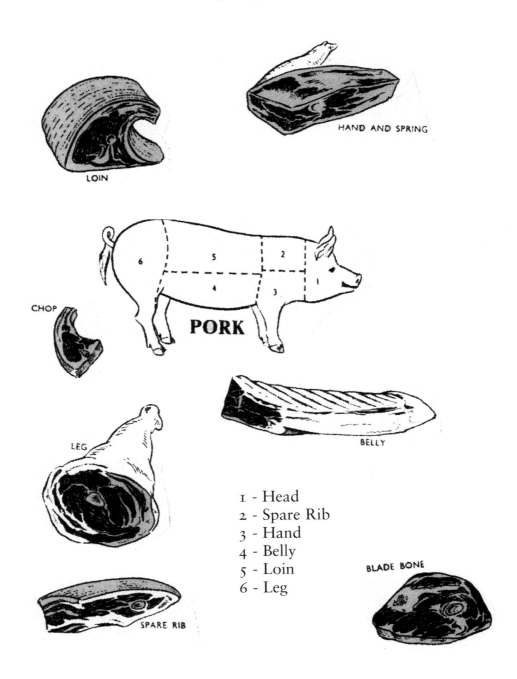

LOIN

HAND AND SPRING

CHOP

PORK

BELLY

LEG

1 - Head
2 - Spare Rib
3 - Hand
4 - Belly
5 - Loin
6 - Leg

BLADE BONE

SPARE RIB

Fred the pig's fate ...

Dee told me many local girls were keen on him, he was considered a good catch. Perhaps it made him keener because I was not chasing him, as all men like a challenge!

When my Dad knew I was driving the horse and float, he showed me the Highway code, in which it demonstrated signals to be made, either by hand or with the whip, to show other road users your intentions. Matt thought it hilarious and I got my leg pulled, but in traffic I did signal properly and felt that I got more respect.

One mid November morning we got the news that Princess Elizabeth had given birth to a son. We were all pleased at the safe arrival and many shop windows dressed up with photographs of the Princess and the Duke of Edinburgh, I tied Prince's mane up with blue ribbon to celebrate.

The farm John worked at was on the phone, but I had to go to the call box near the Seven Stars to phone him. I cycled up there and made my call. On my way back along Fox Lane I was just looking to make the right hand turn across into the drive, when a car roared passed me. How he missed me I do not know. I was left shaking, as his tail lights disappeared up the road. If I had been a cat I would have thought I had just lost another of my nine lives.

Dee wanted some decorating done, the daughter, Jane's bedroom was on the agenda. Dee asked if I would mind sharing my room, while the painting was going on.

It was a condition of the Land Army, that the girl would not share a bedroom with any member of her employer's family. I thought about it, Matt was very good to work for, my wage was a little more than he needed to pay, I got my envelope on a Friday night, if I had been doing the milk rounds on my own, there would often be an extra ten shilling note for me. I had no objection to them moving Jane's bed into my room. It was like having a little sister, we giggled, she tried on my high heeled shoes, my makeup, we did different hair styles she was nice company.

Christmas was looming and I realised that I had fulfilled the two years' service that I had signed on for in the Land Army. Talking to Matt I told him that for the last two Christmases I had been working away from home, he agreed that I would have some time off. But before that, there were extra deliveries of milk, we had to supplement our production with some from the Milk Dept. at Bamber Bridge, and a churn would be left at the side of the road for us to collect.

Dee was busy dressing poultry, it seemed that farmers' wives had the perk of rearing some poultry of their own, to have extra money. So necks were wrung, feathers were plucked and the poultry orders were delivered. It was not a side of farm life that I cared for. Dee offered to show me how to kill and dress the birds, but I could not have done it.

After the morning milk rounds had been done on the Christmas Eve, I set off for home, leaving little gifts for the children's stockings. My journey soon passed, all my fellow passengers were in happy mood, the bus, then train and bus to Eccles.

The door of our little terraced house opened off the pavement into the front room. Quietly letting myself in, I found everywhere dressed up, sprigs, sprays and branches of scarlet berried holly adorned the tops of the pictures and mantle piece, mistletoe was strategically hung over doorways. The sideboard glowed with a bowl of fruit, tangerines and those lovely Canadian apples, Macintosh Reds, each one polished till it shone like a ruby and looking indeed too good to eat. There was a bowl of nuts and a long slim box of dates, a round box of lemon and orange crystallised fruits, things I vaguely remembered from before the war. Then the tray set out with the wine glasses and bottles of port and sherry awaiting the visitors.

As I lifted the latch on the kitchen door, the warm smell of baking wafted to me, Mam was busy making mince pies, she made beautiful pastry. (I have never been able to match it).

Dad had his pint pot of tea and was sampling one of the first batch of pies out of the oven, puffing and blowing to cool it.

Soon I was helping, spooning the mince meat into the pastry lined patty tins, then dredging the baked ones with icing sugar.

Words were not needed. It was Christmas and I was home.

Chapter Twenty
Miss Yellow Belly

In came the New Year 1949, I wondered what it would bring, the winter was cold and biting winds blew sharp as a razor straight across the countryside. The milk froze at times while we were delivering. When we used the van, that was draughty, when using the horse and float, that was open to all the elements, we put the rug over Prince's back. I felt I could have done with a rug too at times. One particularly cold day I left the crate of milk at the cafe and did not stop for a cup of tea, the horse was warm, his breath rose in clouds on the cold air. I wanted to keep him moving. Dave came out to the float and I told him that I did not want to have Prince standing. I liked the way he ran his hand along the arch of Prince's neck, before he patted him and, said 'off you go then.' That little natural gesture told me a lot about Dave's nature, he reminded me of Leo, a man who knew and respected the animals.

Matt used to talk to me about the requirements to go T.T. and getting higher winter production. It was attractive to get a better price for the milk, but he was doubtful as to the red tape, the visiting Milk Recorders and having to keep records. By now I had found that Dee did the book keeping. She did not really want more paperwork.

Although Matt was a youngish chap, in some ways he was old fashioned, in that the bull was 'a man's job'. I would say if I noticed a cow was bulling and he would decide if she was to be served or not. Matt's bull was a Dairy Shorthorn, but not as big an animal as William, and I told Matt that I could help him, as I had handled a bull before, but he insisted that Dee, the children and me were all indoors, while such things were attended to. Whether it was embarrassment or safety, perhaps a little of each.

When it came to calving I did help with that, once I had to lather up and help the cow, as my hands were smaller than Matt's big hands, he reckoned I saved him a vet bill on that one, as we delivered a nice little heifer.

Life settled into a pattern and I had one day off a week when I went home and met John. It seemed to be a lot of travelling, for such a short time together, but it was the best we could do. John had applied for jobs nearer to me, but without success.

The little lads were not well, and were off school, the doctor came and pronounced they had Yellow Jaundice, they were quite poorly, and then Jane became ill with it. Dee moved her back into her old room, after a while when the children were improving, I started to feel ill with awful pains around my waist and back.

I was sick and I was shocked to find that my wee was the colour of tea and motions were nearly white, the doctor came to see me and said that I had got Yellow Jaundice very severely and could expect to be ill for at least six weeks. I could hardly eat anything, things that one would think suitable for a light diet, eggs and milk and dairy produce brought on severe kidney pains. I managed on cornflakes with water.

I lay in bed and felt dreadful, and thought about the forthcoming six weeks. I knew my job would have to be covered and did not wish to make more work for Dee in looking after me. When the doctor came again, he called me Miss Yellow Belly, as I was indeed that colour. I told him I wanted to go home but he said I was too poorly. I wrote to Mam and Dad, and after a few days they came to see me. There was quite a debate, Dee said that she did not want me to go out while I was so ill and she would look after me. However Mam and Dad packed my things and took me home. I never went back to Leyland.

My own doctor came to treat me and I asked him to also have a look at the bottom of my back which had got increasingly painful. My Mam was in the room as chaperone, I think she was quite shocked when the Doctor said that I had damaged the coccyx bone at the base of my spine, he would have to refer me to Eccles and Patricraft Hospital.

I just succumbed to Mam's ministrations, she fussed over me. I was past caring, I just wanted to feel better. Gradually I did.

I had a lot of time to think while I was recuperating, sorting my books and belongings out, I read and re-read the letters Bill had sent me. I wondered where in the world he was and what he was doing now, then put the letters away in the drawer.

I did receive other letters; Dee wrote hoping I was feeling better. I had written to tell them that I understood if they had to replace me. So Matt had taken on a de-mobbed local young man to do my job. Also Dave had asked for my address and she hoped it was all right. They had a new little pig now in the sty, the children called it Fred 2.

The door bell rang, it was a delivery from the local florist, daffodils, narcissus and tulips. They were beautiful and such a wonderful surprise, I had never, ever had flowers sent to me before. Mam said 'John will have sent them', but the card read, 'Hope you are feeling better, I miss my Boadecia, Dave.'

The flowers filled the room with the promise of spring and better times to come, I felt so touched as I arranged them in the big vase, tears rolled down. I knew I would have to acknowledge them and did not know what to do.

My problem was solved when the next post brought a letter from Dave, the gist of it being, that he was sorry I had been ill and heard I would not be returning. Dave said he missed me, the rounds were not fun any more without me to waylay. His father offered me a dairy job at anytime, if I would like to come back to Leyland, they could fix me up with lodgings if I did not want to 'live in'. I let Mam and Dad read the letter, I told them that between the lines, there was a lot more than a job on offer, if I went to work for them it would encourage Dave to court me.

I wrote back thanking Dave for the flowers, and the offer of a job. It was a friendly letter, not wishing to give him false hopes, but I explained that I was not well enough yet to make any plans. When John came on his day off he was very annoyed that another man had sent me flowers.

I had an appointment at the hospital to see Mr Heslop, the surgeon, and when he examined my back he said that I would need an operation to put it right. He would send for me in due course.

Now I was unemployed, drawing one pound six shillings a week benefit. Out of this I gave Mam a pound for my keep. I went to the Labour Exchange, only to find myself in a dilemma, the control of labour was in force. As I had been working in an 'essential job' I just could not leave it to go back into shop work or something that was classed as non-essential. I told them that I was awaiting an operation on my back, but it made no difference. I asked what dairy jobs they had in Eccles Labour Exchange. There were none, but my availability would be circulated around the other Labour Exchanges. Also I was still a member of the Land Army, although I had completed my two years service months ago I had not been discharged.

During this time I saw more of John as I went over on the bus to Wilmslow, we would met at 'The Rex' cinema. Sometimes we saw the film or we would have a cup of tea in the cafe and a stroll round if it was fine.

When I was a child I used to listen to 'Out with Romany' on the 'Children's Hour'. Near the cinema was a piece of land and Romany's caravan (or Vardo he called it) was parked. I think his dog 'Raq' was buried there too.

John and I used to sit on the bench and chat till it was time for me to get the bus back to Manchester. He had ideas of getting his own place, his plans always included me, it was as though it was just taken for granted that we would always be together.

Chapter Twenty-One
Cheesed Off in Cheshire

A letter arrived from the Labour exchange, as they had been notified of a vacancy at one of their Cheshire offices. They had informed the Land Army and hoped I would accept the post on a dairy farm in Cheshire.

Dad looked at the map and we saw I would be only be a few miles miles from Nether Alderly where John was working. He had come some 200 miles north to be near me, now the distance, it seemed, was closing.

I agreed to take the posting. It was the end of March, spring was on its way and so was I. The 15 bus took me to Central Station, (now the G.Mex) where I caught the train, and alighted at the pretty country station with my kit bag. I asked directions and it was only a short distance to the farm. All looked very tidy and well kept, one always goes to the kitchen door, I have yet to see the front door used, on a proper farm. A wall-eyed collie greeted me in the porch, then the door was opened I met Mrs D. As I introduced myself she rather looked down her nose at my well-travelled kit bag, but she ushered me into a huge farm kitchen, with a long table, many chairs and a grandfather clock. There was a big black range at the far end of the room, and she took me up to my room to unpack. When I came down she asked me to help her with the evening meal, I set the table and cut the bread and butter (wondering if Dee's boys were still jockeying for who got the square ends of the loaf).

Eventually, Mr D and several big sons came in. We all sat at the table, and I was very conscious of the steady tick tock of the Grandfather clock. There was hardly any conversation, everyone seemed to concentrate on eating. It was an awful contrast to other mealtimes I had known. Mrs D asked me to clear the table and then to wash up the pots and pans in the back kitchen.

Everyone had drawn their chairs up near the range and I joined them. I started to ask as to what breed of cows they kept and how many milkers they had, was it hand or machine? Looking over the top of his paper Mr D gave me to understand that I would not be involved with the milking and Mrs D would show me my duties. My back was sore to sit on the hard chair and I felt tired, so I excused myself, asking what time did we get up in the mornings and took refuge in my little room. Wondering what kind of a place this was going to be, I went to bed.

Quarter to six Mr D was knocking at my bedroom door, I dodged into the bathroom for a quick wash, between the menfolk using it, dressed and came downstairs into the kitchen. Mr D told me to make a brew of tea for the men and get the range lit, before Mrs D came down. I did manage to get the fire drawing well by the time Mrs D. appeared. Rashers of bacon were put in front of the fire on a trivet arrangement, and I had to set the table, then I was given a bucket containing about 20 pounds of potatoes, a sharp knife and sent to an outhouse to peel them. Across the yard I could hear the rattle and the clatter of machines and buckets, I was eager to get involved but plodded on peeling till I had done all the potatoes. The milk lorry arrived and the menfolk got the churns loaded.

I broke the silence at breakfast time, by asking what work I was supposed to be doing. Mr D said that I was to help the missus. I said that I was trained to do dairy work, and that was what I had understood was to be my job. I was met with a wall of silence. Washing up the breakfast pots, Mrs D came into the back kitchen and started to prepare food for the day's meals. I knew I had to tackle her, I said that I did not mind helping out, but I had come to their farm understanding it would be for dairy work.

She must have been in a talkative mood as I gathered that they had a Displaced Person working far them, an Italian girl Anna, she had just left to go home. Now Anna must have been a paragon of domesticity, she cooked, cleaned, sewed, knitted, did beautiful embroidery and to top it all she had time in the mornings to go to fetch the paper! It appeared that I lagged far behind Anna. Also, had I something more suitable to wear in the house? I had come in my uniform and had working clothes, dungarees and milking coats with me.

Apparently Mrs D had phoned the Local Labour Exchange asking for a girl, and rather like 'Chinese Whispers' by the time the 'vacancy' arrived at Eccles Labour Exchange they thought they had done well to get me placed on a dairy farm.

I told Mrs D that the Land Army did not provide girls to do domestic work. Most girls would have packed up and left then, but I had been without a job and had arranged to meet John the next night, so perhaps the situation could be resolved. During that day I helped with the meals and the washing, the best part was going outside to hang the washing on the lines, the air was warm and a lovely southerly wind was blowing. I filled all the lines and then was told to drape the rest of the clothes over the hedges to dry. Among the hedgerow I found a blackbird building her nest. I would keep her secret and wished her well.

I did ask if I could use the phone to make a call, but was told I had to use the call-box in the village. That evening I tried writing in my room, but the light was poor. I went down to the kitchen and sat at the table; the family were in another room and I was glad of the time to myself. Firstly, I wrote to my W.L.A. local Office informing them of the situation. Then I wrote home, saying I had arrived alright and would see them at the weekend. I did not wish to bother them at this stage and I would try to fight my own battles.

My third letter was to Lorna, my Conway Stewart pen raced along the lines page after page, expressing my frustration and disappointment with this situation. I knew that the post man would collect them in the morning from the kitchen table, but I preferred to put my letters in the village post box myself.

The next day was no better, I was set to clean the bedrooms and bathroom, as well as helping with the meals and peeling the bucket of potatoes. I was annoyed that I had been so misled into coming here. That evening I was getting ready to go out, Mrs D seemed to expect me to do some ironing, but I said I had arranged to meet my boyfriend. John cycled to the village and we sat in the local pub to talk. He was shocked when I told him the situation, as he had been so hoping that I would like the posting. He walked me back to the farm and then went to cycle the miles back. He knew I was on the verge of packing up and going back home.

The next day brought the routine of lighting the range, putting the bacon to cook, peeling the bucket of potatoes. After breakfast I felt utterly humiliated, as Mrs D gave me some sheets of newspaper, boot polish and brushes and rows of boots and shoes to clean. I had to scrape the muck and mud off them with an old knife and clean them before they could be polished. Never in my life had I cleaned anyone else's shoes. How I kept my tongue between my teeth I do not know, especially when Mrs D commented that they were not done as well as Anna did them. I was rapidly getting fed up with Anna.

I was outside cleaning the windows, when the 'cavalry arrived' in the shape of a tweedy lady riding a 'sit up and beg' bicycle. It was my Representative from the Land Army in response to my letter. She greeted me; 'Hello, you must be Miss Cross.'

She breezed up to the door as Mrs D was coming out to see who I was talking to. Before long four of us were sitting at the kitchen table,

Mr and Mrs D on one side, me at the other and my 'knight in shining armour' took the head of the table. This was to check on my welfare and that everyone was happy with the arrangement. I was asked about my room and the food, which I said were good. I noticed Mrs D smile at that. Was my time off agreeable ? I said that I would be going home at weekends, as far as I knew! Mrs D did not smile at that, then the Rep delivered a body blow, 'I am sure you are pleased to have Miss Cross, she comes with excellent references being experienced in hand and machine milking and dairy work'. The tick of the grandfather clock seemed to fill the silence in the room. I did not know if I should speak, but knew I had been given this opening and found myself saying that there seemed to have been some misunderstanding as I had not set foot in the cow sheds, I was not doing any milking, dairying, calf rearing or indeed any farm work at all.

The rep looked at the Ds. 'Is this right? Well, what is the girl doing here?' Mr D blustered, 'helping the missus in the house'.

The W.L.A. Rep sat back aghast. 'Helping in the house?' She then told them that either I did work on the farm or I would have to be removed. It was unfortunate that I had been sent by the Labour Exchange, when what they really required was a live in domestic help.

The outcome was that I was asked if I would take on the poultry combined with 'a little' domestic work. I asked how the hens were kept, as I refused to work in a hen battery. Mr D said the hens were out on the fields in cabins. I asked how long it would take to attend to the poultry. He replied 'best part of the day'. I was still not very happy, but the Rep asked if she could talk to me outside a moment. Her suggestion was that I stay for a week or two and she would offer me the very next dairy posting that came available in the area. If it had not been for trying to be near John, I would have packed my bag and left then.

After the Rep left it was an uneasy atmosphere. Dinnertime was a very unhappy affair for me, the old grandfather clock seemed to be the only friendly sound in that kitchen. I asked what work I had to do with the poultry, and the youngest son said he would show me. We got buckets from the out buildings to carry the corn and feed, we went down the fields.

There were several cabins on the fields and some smaller houses which could be moved about. I told him that I had never dealt with poultry. He showed me where the feed was put in hoppers and to check they had water, while the hens were busy feeding we went and collected the eggs. I got interested in the different hens and was told their flocks were Light Sussex and Rhode Island Reds.

We chatted and I said that my last employer had a hen battery and I thought it cruel to keep hens like that, to which he agreed. Asking what other jobs I had done, he was surprised that I had worked at Merrist Wood, as a friend of his was a student there. He could not understand how I had come to be sent to their place, as he said 'Mother thinks that things have gone back to how they were before the war, and she can get a girl to live in and be in service'.

He said that he would see cabins were cleaned out, but if I could let the hens out first thing in a morning, feed them, collect the eggs, and once again late afternoon, then lock them up at dusk to keep them safe. I had a feeling there was a lot more to keeping poultry than that, but it was a start. When I took the eggs back in the buckets I had to wipe the eggs clean with a soft damp cloth, then they were stacked two dozen at a time on cardboard trays.

I found it took me about 50 minutes to see to the hens in the morning, this put back my potato peeling, but I still had to do it. Afternoon was best, I liked to go down the fields to the hens. Locking the hens up at dusk was not really a perk, as it was done in what should have been my own time. In all it only took up about three hours of my day. This still left a lot of hours at the house.

I kept to wearing my breeches with a nice cream shirt, I felt it something of a statement that I was a Land Army Girl first and foremost and not Mrs D's drudge.

Meeting John at the pub, he was full of news, he had been out working on the fields driving the tractor. John was an 'all rounder' and was willing and able to turn his hand to most farm jobs. The farmer's wife had been doing the dairy and it was being suggested that they get someone to do that work. John understood that his farmer was going to apply for a Land Girl.

I was told not to light the range Friday morning as it had to be cleaned. The black lead and emery paper were provided by the Ds, the elbow grease was mine. I cleaned out the flues and dampers, then I lit the range. I did not have long to admire my handiwork, as Mrs D found fault, I bit my tongue, again hugging to myself the thought that I might never, ever have to do it again, if there was a posting winging its way to me.

I did not ask, I told Mrs D that I was going home Saturday dinnertime and would be back Sunday evening. My Mam and Dad were furious when I told them what work I was doing, they did not want to let me go back 'skivvying'. Dad said he would go to see Mr and Mrs D and collect my things. It was so very tempting, but as I said it could all work out in the coming week. I could be offered the job at the same farm as John and I did not wish to jeopardise that.

Reluctantly I went back Sunday evening, taking with me my clean washing and a light bulb. When I got into my room I climbed up and put in the stronger bulb, that brightened things up a bit, now at least I could see to read and to write my letters.

Next morning as I went about my chores, I kept an eye out for the postman, but there was nothing for me. The day seemed to drag, I have known many a month fly happily by, than a wretched day spent there. The next day's post brought a brown envelope for me, the W.L.A Rep was offering me a post at a dairy farm at Nether Alderly. I told Mrs D that I had to make an urgent phone call, and was off to the village call box. Speaking to the Rep I said that I would be glad to take the posting and it was at C—— Farm where John was working.

The Rep said if I could see the rest of the week out with the Ds while she arranged my transfer. Somehow I got through the day and the I think the hens had an early night, as I could hardly wait to meet John. I knew as soon as I saw him, apparently his farmer was not willing to accept me, simply because I was John's girl friend. He was not going to have any 'messing about under his roof.' John had offered to go into lodgings if that would solve the situation.

The sit up and beg bike brought the Rep to see me again next morning, I spoke to her out in the yard, she said that John's employer could not be persuaded to take me on, she had spoken to him and he was adamant. John was a good worker and he did not want him 'distracted.'

I explained to the Rep that John and I worked well together, we had been at Merrist Wood under the same roof, also I felt it very insulting to my reputation not to be trusted to behave. She quite agreed but did not think he was going to change his mind. Perhaps another posting would come in soon. She would give me priority.

I even phoned John's employer myself and had a chat but to no avail.

I cannot describe my disappointment, I felt so under valued, I had won my spurs through that terrible Winter of 46–47 at Limpsfield. I had learned my job and although young, had been given responsibility and treated with respect at Merrist Wood. At Leyland, Matt had treated me as a friend and one of the family, at times he even took notice of my suggestions. I knew that I could not stay here, every mealtime was a trial, no matter how well I did a job, it was not satifactory, in fact I was very unhappy.

Mr and Mrs D were going out, but I was left with plenty of instructions, one being to scrub the kitchen floor. As soon as they went I set about my chores, tidied the range, dusted, then I came to the grandfather clock, how old he was I do not know, pondering on what times he had steadily tick tocked his way through, the moon dial peeping through the painted clouds showed me a smiling face. I smiled back and gave him an extra polish, then set about cleaning what seemed to be acres of red tiled floor. All looked clean and polished as I set off to feed the hens.

That was my treat of the day, the further away from the house the better. I loved the stroll down the fields, the hens were getting to know me now and gathered round as I fed them. There were two cockerels, they did a little sparring up to each other and I called them Rommel and Monty. I was also learning where some hens hid their eggs, and I had to search in the corners of the cabins. Bringing the eggs back up to the house, an idea came in my head that if I got the eggs done before Mr and Mrs D returned, I would present myself at the cow sheds and see if I could do some milking. 'Just to keep my hand in', and who knows maybe I would be able to prove my worth.

As I was wiping and traying up the eggs, they came back. Mrs D came to the outbuilding, she was not satisfied with the kitchen floor, telling me that she knew it had been mopped, not scrubbed. I said I had knelt and scrubbed the floor, if she did not believe me look at the mop, it was dry. There was some remark about me having an answer for everything and would I come and help with tea.

Next morning there was some activity in the farm yard, the men were marking out a large circle, I gathered that they were planning on erecting a silo for silage. On going to do the afternoon feeding, I saw the youngest son was working with a tractor and trailer cleaning out the cabins. We chatted and he laughed when he heard me refer to Rommel and Monty. We started talking about silage, it was the first time they had decided to make some. I said it was good rich winter feed and the cows loved it. I did remark on the wisdom of building a silo in the yard, especially with the prevailing south-west wind behind it. I explained that silage in the making had a very sickly smell that permeated everywhere, and again when it was opened up to be used, the fermenting green crop and the molasses gave off a very pungent smell. It was not something I would have too near the house.

That evening I heard discussion between the men folk, regarding the site for the silo. Mr D over ruled them saying he wanted it close by the cows for feeding. I hoped that in the months to come Mrs D would agree with him. Do you know, that thought cheered me a little.

That night I tossed and turned, I woke up and was itching all over, I got up and looked in the bed and examined the sheets wondering if I had picked up same mites or fleas off the poultry. I had a rotten uncomfortable night, the next morning I found I had some spots on my body. By breakfast time they had spread to my neck. I told Mrs D that I thought I had better go home, she had a look at the spots and said that she thought I better had, as it looked as though I had chickenpox adding that thankfully all her family had it when they were small.

Chickenpox was a small price to pay to escape, I felt the decision had been made for me, as I threw all my belongings into my kit bag, I knew that I would not return.

On taking my leave of Mrs D, I told her not to keep the job open for me as the arrangement was not really satisfactory to either of us. She nodded, I think we understood one another.

Then I was heading for the station, I did not know the time of the next train, nor did I care, preferring to sit at the station, rather than spend another moment at that place.

Afterwards

Where I had got the chickenpox from, I never knew, I saw my doctor as I needed a sick note, he examined my back again and said that I had abscesses on my spine. What with that and the jaundice, I was so run down, I was catching everything that was going.

By the beginning of May I went into Eccles and Patricroft Hospital. I had nothing but praise for our new National Health Service. Mr Heslop was a good surgeon. I was treated with the new wonder drug, penicillin. I felt like a pin cushion, having injections every four hours, night and day, my bottom, my arms, my thighs. I had to lie on my tummy all the time. I survived on drinks and had nothing to eat for ten days, so that everything healed down below. One of my school friends, Mabel, who had gone into nursing had the honour of removing my stitches. I was in hospital for three weeks.

I remember asking Mr Heslop would the operation affect me as regards 'other things'. He laughed and reassured me, and wrote a note on his prescription pad, which he tucked in my dressing gown pocket. When I looked at it, I smiled as the three items prescribed, were that I get married, have a family and enjoy life.

I think that was the best prescription ever I had.

The month of June and haymaking, but it found me staying for two weeks, free of charge, at a Convalescent Home run by the Health Service at Trinity Square, Llandudno.

Once again I was thrown in with an assorted group of women and girls, considering we were all re-couperating we really enjoyed ourselves. I was in a group that needed 'building up' and Matron weighed us when we arrived and once again when we left. If we had not put on at least five pounds Matron took it as a slight on her care and was very disappointed in the offenders. We had to have a glass of milk mid morning, so we could not go far; perhaps a stroll along Mostyn Street looking at the shops. After dinner we got the bus in

Trinity Square to Deganway where they had a 'Lido' and a poolside cafe, here we met up with the patients of the Men's Convalescent Home. We were a very motley crew and I realised how much I had missed fun, sing songs and laughter lately.

On the middle Saturday we were asked if we would 'volunteer' to take collection boxes out on the streets for The St John's Ambulance Brigade. I was friendly with Barbara, so off we went all along the prom. I soon found that if you smiled and rattled the collecting tin, young men would come over and give very generously if we pinned their flags on for them. Many half crowns and even a ten shilling note was donated. We had to come back for our mid morning milk, but our collecting tins were full and we had run out of flags. Matron kindly replenished our supplies and we headed off with empty tins in the direction of the Pier. Returning for dinner, we asked to go out again in the afternoon,

Llandudno, June 1949.
The author and Barbara collecting for St. John's Ambulance

as I said to Matron, new visitors were coming in, and we covered the railway station. I think Matron was quite amused at our enthusiasm.

A week later I got off the train at Eccles station. Mam and Dad said how well and sun tanned I looked, also I had met Matron's requirement of putting on a little weight, my back was very tender for a very long time after, but I was getting well again!

A visit to the Labour Exchange and I found things were more relaxed, I could take other work, they offered me a job at a ladies' dress shop, which I accepted for the time being, it only paid two pounds a week but it was a stop gap, at least I was earning my keep.

I had a lot of time for thinking while I had been ill, I knew I had big decisions to make. I realised how John had changed, when we first went to the Dairy Show we laughed a lot, at Merrist our relationship was fun, but now he was so very serious. I told him that I did not like the way we were now and I wanted to finish. John said he would not give me up, we had come through a rough time and things would get better now. So we limped along together for a little while longer, but in my heart I knew it was over.

Going through my things I read the letter and card Dave had sent me, did I want to go back to dairy work? Did I want to go back to Leyland? Did I want to get involved with Dave?

A letter from Lorna arrived, she was coming up to Liverpool to visit her family. I went over on the Sunday. Lorna had been accepted for Agricultural College and would be starting there in October. She asked me to apply for the college too, and we could do the course together. She also brought the message that Mr Hunt would be pleased employ me again, if I wished to return.

Then there were Bill's lovely letters, his private thoughts that he had penned when he had been off watch. As I re-read them, I thought that at the time I should have been braver, I certainly had never felt about anyone else as I did about him. I had his home address and so many times I sat and wrote. Then I thought that perhaps he was married now, I did not wish to make a bigger fool of myself, so my letters were never posted. I left one on my dressing table sealed and stamped, half hoping that Mam would post it for me, but eventually it went the way of the others on the kitchen fire.

A letter arrived from the W.L.A. hoping I was recovered and asking if I still want to be offered a dairy posting. Or I could have an 'Honourable Discharge' as I had more than filled my contract. That was an easier decision to make; I would take my discharge knowing I could get myself a dairy job with the contacts I had.

I had to send my uniform and badge back, I did return the things I had been issued with, as that entitled me to some clothing coupons. I was still left with a good wardrobe, as I had bought plenty of clothes when I was at Guildford. I kept them in case I went back dairying.

It made me sad at having to return my badge, I often thought that we should have been allowed to keep them. I know I had always worn mine with pride.

The original Women's Land Army badge

Dad was in the back yard looking at my bike, it had been covered with tarpaulin to keep it dry. It was like seeing an old friend again, we set about cleaning it and pumping up the tyres. What memories it stirred, riding the highways and byways, the rutted icy roads, dusty lanes, through the woods, even over fields to bring the cows in. It had been my trusty steed, I had even carried milk cans on my handlebars. We soon had it all clean and shining again, Dad asked what I wanted to do with my bike as I was still not able to ride it. So we advertised and I got a fair price of eight pounds. We threw in the pump, saddlebag, lamps and Dad clinched the deal when he included an ex-army signal lamp. This was a standby as it showed three colours, white that could be used as a torch or as a headlight, the red was a spare or extra rear light. I watched as a young lady rode my bike away and wondered what further adventures it would have.

I needed a new coat as styles had changed and the 'New Look' had brought in mid calf length. While working at the dress shop I chose myself a coat from the wholesalers; it was a lovely shade of blue, very smart and much admired. The money from my bike was well spent.

I applied for a job at the Eccles Co-operative Society, as they paid the best shop wages, I had to sit an exam which was easy enough, just little sums, reckoning up, some on pints and quarts, weights and measures, the manager commented that not many girls got all the later sums right. He told me that when they had a vacancy they would let me know.

I decided to end my relationship with John, we had known each other nearly two years. There was so much talk, about still being friends and keeping in touch, but I wanted to finish completely. I received a lovely letter from John's mother, and John wrote to my parents. I did not change my mind and I made a clean break.

In a strange way it was a relief; I felt free to go out with the girls from work, and I often went to the pictures with my cousin John. Then a letter arrived offering me a job at the Eccles Co-Op, if I was willing to take a position in the Drapery Department at Urmston. I accepted and started beginning of October, just before my twentieth birthday.

Each morning I caught the 22 bus out of Eccles Bus station, a young man that worked in the Furnishing Department, caught the bus at Barton Lane he started to sit next to me.

We went on our first date in November and by Christmas he had proposed.

Dear Len, 'my love' for the rest of my life.

Before I married Len, I burnt Bill's letters, I watched the flames lick round them, then the burnt corners curled into ash and everything was gone.

Lorna went to College, there she met and married a fellow student, William Whyte. When Len and I were married we were invited over to Liverpool one Sunday to Mr and Mrs Jackson's as Lorna and her husband were over on a visit. They had a lovely little daughter.

That was the last time Lorna and I were together. I have tried 'Lost Touch' and 'Reunited' but without success so far.

Liverpool, 1951. The last time Lorna and the author were together

Postscript

The Womens Land Army disbanded in 1950, their job was done.

Men had left the farms to go into the fighting services, women and girls came forward to replace them. We did our best, helping to feed the Country, producing food, harvesting crops, milking, supplying timber to re-build homes. It was heavy, dirty work for young women.

To be a 'Land Girl' you needed a sense of humour, be able to improvise, ready to tackle anything and know how to enjoy the simplest of pleasures, like hot water and scented soap. We had a great spirit of comradeship, pride in the work we did, most of us had an inbred love of the countryside and the animals that shared our lives

Every Land Girl has her own story to tell, this has been mine.

Words to Land Army Songs

For a good sing-song

If you want to go to heaven when you die
You should wear a green pulllover and a tie
And a little khaki bonnet, with W.L.A. on it
If you want to go to heaven when you die
Singing, I will, if you will, so will I
Singing, I will if you will, so will I
Singing, I will, if you will. I will if you will, I will if you will
So will I

(to the tune of She'll be Coming Round the Mountain*)*.

—

This one carried a warning

Around her neck she wore a yellow ribbon,
She wore it in the springtime,
In the merry month of May, (hey hey)
And if you asked her why the heck shewears it
She wears it for the feller feller who is far, far away

Around the town she pushed a baby carriage
She pushed it in the springtime,
In the merry month of May, (hey, hey)
And if you ask her why the heck she pushed it
She pushed it for that feller, who was far, far away

Behind the door her father keeps a shotgun
He keeps it in the springtime,
In the merry month of May (hey, hey)
And if you ask him why the heck he keeps it
He keeps it for that yankee, who is far, far away

———

This is a nonsense song with many verses; it fitted into a suza march

Have a care for your web-footed friend,
For a duck may be somebody's mother
She lives in a marsh or a swamp (pomp, pomp)
Where the weathers always damp
You may think this the end of my song
Well it is
But I will sing you another

———

This one was a favourite when a romance had come to an end

When you met somebody new,
Someone who appeals to you
I'll wish you all the luck in the world

I won't be a clinging vine
You go your way, I'll go mine
And wish you all the luck in the world

And if I see her with you,
I'll understand
I'll try to smile as I take her hand

And when they play 'here comes the bride'
I'll be waiting, just outside.
To wish you all the luck in the world

This was a sad, whistful song; it referred to the Australians landing at the dardenelles

In an old Australian homestead,
With the ivy round the door
A girl received a letter,
It had just come from the war
With her mother's arm around her,
She gave way to grief and sighs
As she read that sad, sad letter,
The tears fell from her eyes
'Why do I weep, why do I pray?
My love has gone, so far away.
He played his part, that August day
And left my heart, in Suvla Bay

—

The Oxen — by Thomas Hardy

Christmas Eve, and twelve of the clock.
'Now they are on their knees'
An elder said as we sat in a flock
By the embers in hearthside ease.

We pictured the meek mild creatures where
They dwelt in their strawy pen,
Nor did it occur to one of us there
To doubt they were kneeling then.

So fair a fancy few would weave
In these years! Yet I feel,
If someone said on Christmas Eve,
'Come see the oxen kneel'.

'In the lonely barton, by yonder coomb
Our chidhood used to know'
I should go with him in the gloom
Hoping it might be so.

Poems of the time

Have I lingered here before – and gazed on parish spires
From this windy hill top – seen those blue distant shires?

Was I once a country lass? Skirts hoisted to my knees
Running in the meadow – talking to the bees?

Did I know the warmth of cows? Milk frothing in the pail
And, in that time, did I bake and brew a nutty ale?

Did I have my own pet hen? Her eggs twin yoked and brown
Have I sat beside this brook? Seen the water tumble down

Have I been 'a Maying'? With flowers in my hair
Or joined the happy folk at Michaelmas Fair

And did I laugh and love before – in that dim long a while
Did I keep an evening tryst? Down by the rustic stile

Was I once a country lass? Akin to this earth rich and brown
Long ago, before I was claimed and captured by the town

Was I once a country lass, was it ever me?

Abendlied (Der Tag mit seinem Lichte)

We thank you, Lord of Heaven,
For all the joys that greet us,
For all that you have given,
To help and delight us
In earth and sky and seas;
The sunlight on the meadows,
The rainbow's fleeting wonder
The clouds with cooling shadows,
The stars that shine in splendour –
We thank you lord for these.

For swift and gallant horses,
For lambs in pastures springing
For dogs with friendly faces,
For birds with music thronging
Their chantries in the trees;
For herbs to cool our fever,
For flowers of field and garden,
For bees among the clover
With stolen sweetness laden –
We thank you, Lord, for these.

For homely dwelling places
Where childhood's visions linger,
For friends and kindly voices,
For bread to stay our hunger
And sleep to bring us ease;
For zeal and zest of living,
For faith and understanding,
For words to tell our loving,
For hope of peace, unending –
We thank you, Lord, for these.

Epilogue

Celebrating the achievements of the Land Girls

My dear granddaughter, there you are; eager and ready to fly the nest, off to university. Full of love, life, fun and such high hopes. I vividly recall when I was younger than you are now, when I too wanted to spread my wings and do something worthwhile.

It was then that I was one of the 80,000 girls that joined the Women's Land Army. We always were a Cinderella service, mostly because we were scattered around the countryside, either in small groups living in hostels or on individual farms. Some of our number fought to get recognition and, at the millennium, won the right to have a contingent proudly join the March Past at the Cenotaph.

Our number dwindle as the years take their toll, but when it was decided that a badge was to be awarded, some 28,000 ladies applied. In July 2008, the postman brought me a little box containing a certificate and the badge. This was followed by two invitations: the first to take place at our local Civic Centre on 5 November 2008, with the other to be held at Manchester Town Hall on 7 November.

At the celebration held at the Civic centre, we were each presented with a certificate by the deputy Mayor. A delightful afternoon tea was served and we were soon chatting away, exchanging memories and laughing. Although one or two wheelchairs and a few walking sticks were in evidence, my youngest son, Steve, who had escorted me, commented that we were a sprightly lot, with a twinkle in the eye! This celebration was the warm-up for the much larger celebration at Manchester Town Hall.

Arriving by taxi with my friend, Alan – I had an R.A.F. escort – we were met on the Town Hall steps and right away were made to feel special. Directed to the lift, our coats were taken care of and we joined the other guests for a welcoming cup of tea. The proceedings were very well organised and we had a lovely afternoon. A screen was showing old photographs, we each had a souvenir programme and a Union Jack flag. We had a welcome speech from the Lord Mayor of Manchester and a message from Her Majesty, the Queen, by the Lord-Lieutenant of Greater Manchester, Warren J. Smith J. P.

An act of worship was led by the Rector of St Ann, Manchester; the Reverend Nigel Ashworth, followed by music of the era. There were renditions of many of Ivor Novello's lovely songs with Diana Palmerston, Aled Wyn Davis and Eirian Owen at the piano. When it came to the community singing, I think we could have rivalled the Albert Hall, especially when we finished with *Land of Hope and Glory*, waving our flags aloft.

We retired for refreshments, where around 600 of us were served.

Although I did not meet any girls (for girls we will always be) that I knew, it seemed as though we shared so much. We were chatting about the rough conditions we had endured and the spirit of us all being in it together – I caught many scraps of others' conversations:

'I only had a hat and an armband when I was sent to a farm in Cornwall.'

'Well I took one look at the bull serving the cow; it put me off men for years!'

'I had chilblains on my fingers from picking sprouts in the frost.'

'I got wet through cutting the kale.'

'Did you do threshing? What a filthy job that was.'

'Riding the bikes around the lane, we only had one lamp between us.'

So the echoes of those days spanned the sixty years that had past. I wondered what had become of my friends Sylvia, Jane, Pat and Lorna and where life had taken them.

Amid the splendour of Manchester Town Hall, I remembered the harsh winters, the glorious summers, the friends I had worked with, the patient cattle, the little calves and the cats, the dogs and horses that had shared my life.

It was an experience I would not like to have missed.

November 2008.

Manchester Town Hall

To celebrate the lives and work of the Greater Manchester

Land Girls

&

The Timber Corp

Friday 7th November 2008

The front cover of the souvenir programme.

Dear Mrs A Bagnall

A CELEBRATION OF THE WOMEN'S LAND ARMY AND TIMBER CORPS

Manchester Town Hall, Albert Square, Manchester M60 2LA
7th November at 1.30pm

The Department for Environment, Food and Rural Affairs (DEFRA), supported by the office of the Prime Minister's Office, have asked the Lord-Lieutenants of England and Scotland to arrange a celebration to mark the work of the Women's Land Army and Timber Corps.

The Lord-Lieutenant of Greater Manchester, Mr Warren Smith, and the Lord Mayor of Manchester, Councillor Mavis Smitheman, have asked me to write to you personally and to invite you to join them at Manchester Town Hall on 7th November 2008.

The event will begin at 1.30pm with a short service in the Great Hall followed by music and singing from the 1940's and beyond. Afternoon Tea will be available from approximately 2.30pm and the event will conclude at 3.30pm.

I do realise that you may well wish to bring someone with you and this person would be most welcome; disabled access is available throughout the building.

To help with catering arrangements I would be grateful if you would complete and return the slip at the bottom of the page. I do hope that you will be able to join us as we come together to recognise the significant work done by these women during those trying times.

Yours sincerely,

The author's invitation to the celebration

With the country at war and all able-bodied men needed to fight against the forces of Germany, there was a shortage of labour to work on farms and in other key jobs on the land. At the same time it was becoming increasingly difficult to get food imported from abroad, so more land needed to be farmed to provide home-grown food. It was the Women's Land Army that provided much of the labour force to work this land and feed our nation. The advertising slogan read: 'For a healthy, happy job join the Women's Land Army'. In reality, the work was hard and dirty and the hours were too long. Some of the girls received training before they were sent to farms; the farmers themselves trained others. The Timber Corps was set up to teach women to make pit props, necessary for working in mines, which then had to be loaded onto lorries and transported to the mining areas.

The girls of the Land Army looked after animals, ploughed the fields, dug up potatoes, harvested the crops, killed the rats, dug and hoed for 48 hours a week in the summer. As there was not enough machinery to go round they often had to work with old-fashioned equipment, such as horse-drawn hand ploughs and to harvest crops by hand. Of course, all this heavy outdoor work made them very hungry. One advantage was that extra rations were allocated to farm workers to give them the energy they needed to farm the land.

Piece from the programme concerning the Women's Land Army

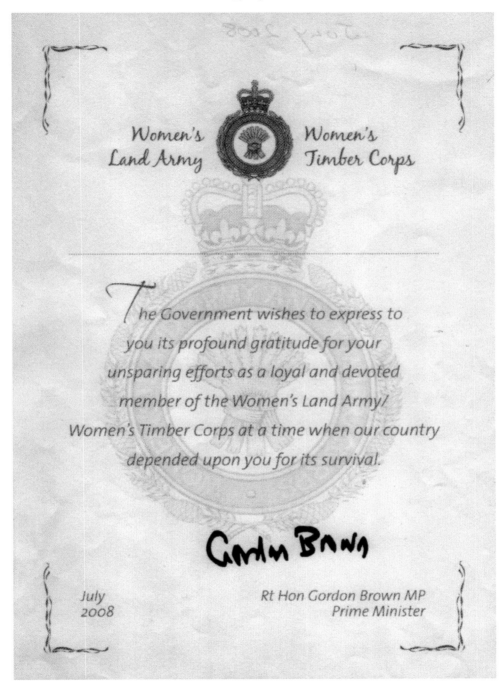

Women's
Land Army

Women's
Timber Corps

The Government wishes to express to
you its profound gratitude for your
unsparing efforts as a loyal and devoted
member of the Women's Land Army/
Women's Timber Corps at a time when our country
depended upon you for its survival.

Gordon Brown

July
2008

Rt Hon Gordon Brown MP
Prime Minister

The author's certificate from the Prime Minister, thanking her for her efforts in the Women's Land Army

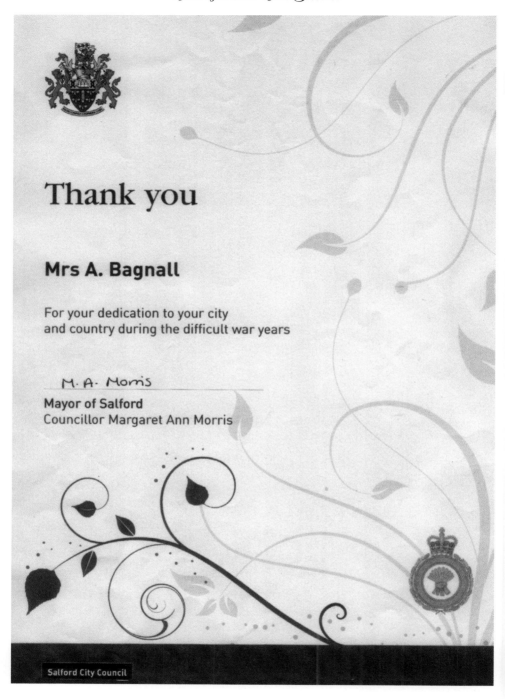

Thank you

Mrs A. Bagnall

For your dedication to your city
and country during the difficult war years

M. A. Morris

Mayor of Salford
Councillor Margaret Ann Morris

Salford City Council

The author's certificate from the Mayor of Salford

The presentation badge given to members of the Women's Land Army in 2008

The author, pictured with her certificate and presentation badge in November 2008